NOBLE LESSONS –
Words of Islamic Wisdom

A collection of 20+ Islamic articles based on the guidance of Quran and Hadith to help everyone in their daily lives.

IqraSense.com

"Indeed Allah conferred a great favor on the believers when He sent among them a Messenger (Muhammad) from among themselves, reciting unto them His Verses (the Quran), and purifying them (from sins by their following him), and instructing them (in) the Book (the Quran) and Al-Hikmah [the wisdom and the Sunnah (traditions) of the Prophet (i.e. his legal ways, statements, acts of worship)], while before that they had been in manifest error."

-- (Quran, Surah Aal-e-Imran, Verse #164)

IqraSense.com

Library of Congress Cataloging-in-Publication Data 2014921462
CreateSpace Independent Publishing Platform, North Charleston, SC

Copyright © 2015 IqraSense.com

All rights reserved. No part of this book may be reproduced, in any form or by any means, without permission in writing from the publisher and authors at IqraSense.com.

Printed in the United States of America

ISBN: 1505264502
ISBN-13:   978-1505264500

To report any errors or for any other inquiries, please write to admin@IqraSense.com

Other Books by IqraSense.com

1. The Power of Du'a (Prayers)
2. 100+ Du'a (Prayers) for Success and Happiness
3. Jesus – The Prophet Who Didn't Die
4. Inspirations from the Quran - Selected DUAs, Verses, and Surahs from the Quran
5. Summarized Stories of the Qur'aan
6. Healing and Shifa from Quran and Sunnah: Spiritual Cures for Physical and Spiritual Conditions based on Islamic Guidelines
7. Jerusalem: A Religious History – The Centuries Old Christian, Islamic, and Jewish struggle for the "Holy Lands"

TABLE OF CONTENTS

1. INTRODUCTION 11

2. UNDERSTANDING AND HANDLING LIFE'S DIFFICULTIES AND CALAMITIES 17

2.1 A Muslim's Attitude Toward Challenges and Difficulties 17

2.2 Dealing with Life's Challenges and Difficulties 21

3. KEEPING A STRONG FAITH DURING TOUGH TIMES 28

3.1 Do Not Feel Helpless 28

3.2 Revive Your Faith 30

3.3 Believe in the Divine Decree 31

3.4 Ask for Allah's Mercy for an Out from Tough Situations 32

3.5 Stay Patient in Hard Times 33

3.6 Remember Allah in Good Times 34

4. MATTERS OF THE (MUSLIM) HEART 36

5. TAKING STOCK OF OUR "THINKING" ABILITIES 41

6. ALIGNING OUR TIME TO LIFE'S PURPOSE 46

6.1 Be Mindful Of Your Purpose In This Life 47

6.2	Become More Action Oriented	48
6.3	Don't Concern Yourself With Unnecessary Matters	50
6.4	Don't Forget The Daily Remembrance Of Allah	51
7.	**THE BLESSINGS OF GRATITUDE AND SHUKR**	**53**
8.	**CORRECTING OTHERS BY "ADVISING" AND NOT "CONDEMNING"**	**59**
8.1	Your Role When Providing Advice	60
8.2	Tips To Consider When Correcting Others	61
8.3	Advising In Personal Situations	64
9.	**RIDDING ONESELF OF JEALOUSY, HATRED, AND RESENTMENT**	**67**
9.1	Feeling Jealous Of Other's Provisions And Rizq	70
9.2	Cleaning Our Hearts Of Jealousy And Hatred	71
10.	**NOT LOSING HOPE IN THE DU'AS THAT WE MAKE**	**72**
11.	**MANAGING RELATIONSHIPS**	**76**
11.1	Some Relationships Can Involve Pain	77
11.2	Relationships Can Be Pleasing And Fulfilling	78
11.3	Relationships Must Be Actively Managed	78
11.4	Prioritize Your Relationships	82

11.5	Relationships Can Be Repaired	84
11.6	Relationships Are Defined By A Person's Character	86
11.7	The Ultimate Relationship Is The One With Our Creator	87
11.8	Use Good Old Common Sense	87

12. THE SIN OF RIYA (SHOWING OFF) 89

12.1	Doing Good Deeds For Worldly Reasons Is Minor Shirk	90
12.2	Punishment in the Hereafter	91
12.3	Punishment in This World	92
12.4	Causes and Cures	93

13. THE ISLAMIC ETIQUETTE OF DEALING WITH PEOPLE....99

13.1	Not Showing Pride And Arrogance	99
13.2	Not Mocking Others	100
13.3	Not Addressing People With Undesirable Titles	101
13.4	Refraining From 'Tajassus' (Spying)	102
13.5	Resolving Differences with People	103
13.6	Controlling Your Hands And Tongue	105
13.7	Attributing Positive Motives To Others' Actions	105
13.8	Expressing Gratitude To Others	106
13.9	Smiling At Others Is Charity	106

13.10	Visiting The Sick	107
13.11	Being Kind, Gentle, Caring And Concerned	107

14. USING "TAWAKKUL" TO RELIEVE OUR ANXIETIES AND WORRIES 109

15. BALANCING BETWEEN "TAWAKKUL" IN ALLAH AND OUR EFFORTS 113

16. THE URGENCY OF PERSONAL CHANGE 117

16.1	Desensitization to Time	118
16.2	Desensitization to Falsehood and Imperfections	119
16.3	Lack of Commitment	121
16.4	Lack of a Personal Change System	122

17. THE NECESSITY OF IKHLAS (SINCERITY) 124

18. TIPS FOR YOUR "MUSLIM MARRIAGE" 128

19. REINFORCING TRAITS OF PERSONAL EXCELLENCE 133

20. ISLAMIC MORALS AND ETIQUETTES 139

21. LIVING ISLAM WITHIN A FAMILY (HOME) 144

21.1	Make Home a Place for The Family to Worship Allah	146
21.2	Keep Satan Out of Your House	148

21.3 Let Respect, Kindness and Trust Rule the Affairs of the Family 150

21.4 Foster a Culture of Islamic Learning and Knowledge 151

21.5 Make Family Decisions Through Mutual Consultation........153

21.6 Understand and Fulfill Responsibilities Toward Other Family Members..154

22. OTHER BOOKS BY IQRASENSE 156

This page is intentionally left blank.

1. Introduction

This book includes a compilation of articles that cover a number of important topics that can help a Muslim believer in his or her daily life. In the light of Islamic guidance from the Quran, Hadith of Prophet Muhammad (sallallahu alaihi wa sallam – may peace and blessings of Allah be upon him), and the explanations of many renowned scholars, these articles can serve as a beacon of light guiding the reader on many life's issues. These include topics on how to handle life's challenges, putting one's trust in Allah, Islamic morals and etiquette, matters related to Muslim marriage, personal relationships, and many others. The following provides a brief synopsis of the various chapters and their contents. The reader should note that these articles have been earlier discussed on the IqraSense Islamic blog as well.

Chapter 2 – Understanding and Handling Life's Difficulties, and Calamities: This chapter explains the role of difficulties, trials, and calamities in a believer's life and the wisdom behind them. The article also covers the rewards associated with handling life's such challenges. The chapter uses Quranic verses and the Prophet's ahadith to elaborate on the concept.

Chapter 3 – Keeping A Strong Faith During Tough Times: This chapter elaborates on handling oneself during tough times and the things that one can do to keep a strong faith in Almighty Allah and His powers. The chapter also provides tips related to keeping ones faith strong and strategies for getting out of problems.

Chapter 4 – Matters of the (Muslim) Heart: Our emotions and decisions in all aspects of our lives are mostly driven by our hearts. Thus, if our heart is good, everything can be good, and vice versa. In this context, this chapter shows the reader the spiritual impact that one's heart can have on our soul and lives in general.

Chapter 5 – Taking Stock of Our "Thinking" Abilities: In the Quran, Allah challenges mankind to "think" and "think deeply". In the light of Quran and Hadith, this chapter relates to that message, and guides us to our thinking and searching for meaning, and how we can enhance our thinking abilities, and the underlying things to keep in mind during our quest for answers.

Chapter 6 – Aligning Our Time to Life's Purpose and Priorities: To help us stay on the right path and to utilize our time in this world to prepare for the eternal life, this chapter guides us on our purpose, priorities, and shows us how we can constructively move forward.

Chapter 7 – The Blessings of Gratitude and Shukr: This chapter emphasizes the need and the rewards associated with thanking our Lord in all situations. It reminds us about Allah's blessings and provisions to us and our obligation for expressing our gratitude and shukr to Him.

Chapter 8 – Correcting Others by Advising and Not Condemning: To ensure we don't ruin our relationships, this chapter reminds us on the evils of condemning others and alternately encourages us to advise people instead when correcting them.

Chapter 9 – Ridding Oneself of Jealousy, Hatred, and Resentment: To help us lead happy lives, this chapter guides us on simple tips that we can follow to clean our hearts from the feelings of jealousy and hatred.

Chapter 10 – Not Losing Hope in the Du'as That we Make: The relationship between the Almighty Allah and us becomes stronger when we ask Allah what we want through the du'as that we make to Him. This chapter discusses the topic of du'as and how they can have a transformative effect on one's life.

Chapter 11 – Managing the Pain and Pleasure of Relationships: Pain and pleasure are part and parcel of our life and relationships. While some relationships can bring us satisfaction and pleasure, others can be painful. This chapter guides us on how to repair our relationships, and how to prioritize them to minimize the pain and maximize the pleasure associated with them.

Chapter 12 – The Sin of Riya: Riya is considered a big sin as the act involves doing things that are pleasing to Allah with the intention of seeking the admiration from people instead. This chapter explains the concept, causes of this sin, and suggests cures on how to protect yourself from committing this act.

Chapter 13 – The Islamic Etiquette of Dealing with People: This chapter targets our social life and teaches us the etiquettes of dealing with others in our daily lives. It includes guidelines on resolving differences, if any, between us and others. It also discusses some important things to make our social life more peaceful and delightful.

Chapter 14 – How to use "Tawakkul" in Relieving our Anxieties and Worries: Tawakkul refers to putting your utmost faith in Almighty Allah. This chapter states the benefits of Tawakkul and explains how one can relieve anxieties and worries by merely using Tawakkul. The explanation includes the associated guidelines referenced from the Quran and Hadith.

Chapter 15 – Balancing Between "Tawakkul" In Allah And Human Efforts: This chapter helps us to further understand the true sense of Tawakkul, and explains how to fashion our behaviors and lives in line with the principles of Tawakkul.

Chapter 16 – The Urgency of Personal Change: This chapter highlights the need for personal change from an Islamic perspective and how we can use this tool to transform our lives for the better in this life and to get ready for the hereafter.

Chapter 17 – The Necessity of Ikhlas (Sincerity): This chapter highlights the importance of sincerity in all our actions. It discusses the need to purify ones intentions and to make ones deeds good in light of Islamic principles.

Chapter 18 – Tips for Your "Muslim Marriage": This chapter provides select guidance on the do's and dont's for married couples in the light of the verses from the Quran and Prophet's ahadith.

Chapter 19 – Reinforcing Traits of Personal Excellence: In this life, we should utilize our capabilities to strive for excellence. This chapter illustrates how we can reinforce our personality traits to seek excellence. It describes how to form strong positive beliefs and how to make our lives more meaningful as a result.

Chapter 20 – Islamic Morals and Etiquettes: The religion of Islam is infused with moral values and etiquettes. This chapter demonstrates these etiquettes and moral values to be observed in all situations. It shows us how one can instill life with these moral values to make lives more meaningful and delightful.

Chapter 21 – Living Islam within a Family (Home): An integral part of our life is our home and family, whose wellbeing is one of our primary concerns. This chapter includes Islamic guidance about living stable and happy lives and states how one can live a prosperous family life staying within the limits of Islam.

Finally, as you read this book, you will notice special phrases inserted after particular names. These are phrases of honor and respect that are reserved for certain classes of individuals, for angels, or for Allah Himself. First and foremost to honor is always Allah, whose name or identifying pronoun may be followed by 'Subhanahu Wa Ta'ala' (SWT), meaning "May He be glorified and exalted." The name of His Prophet, Muhammad is usually followed by the phrase 'sallallahu alaihi wa sallam' (S.A.W.S.), translated as "May Allah send prayers and peace upon him." The names of angels, such as Gabriel (Jibrail) and prophets other than Muhammad (S.A.W.S.) are followed by the phrase 'alaihis salam' (A.S.), meaning "Peace be upon him," or "them," as in this instance. Finally, the prophet's companions' names are followed by the phrase 'radi Allah anhu' (R.A.) translated as "May Allah be pleased with him" for men. For women, 'anha' is used instead of 'anhu'.

Another thing that you will occasionally come across is particular terms relating to the transmission of the hadith. The term *sahih*, for instance, describes the highest standard of authenticity in hadith classification. The most notable compilation of sahih hadith is by Bukhari and Muslim. A musnad is a collection of hadith as well, the most notable being the Musnad of Imam Ahmed Ibn Hanbal. Another term, sunan, the plural of sunnah, is also a collection of hadith but with an emphasis on conduct, ritual, and rules for living as originally practiced and prescribed by the Prophet Muhammad (S.A.W.S.) Finally, the term *tafsir*, which stands for "commentary" or "exegesis," refers to a highly involved science of interpretation whose purpose is to give a more complete explanation of the Qur'aanic verses through reference to both the Surahs (chapters of the Qur'aan) and to other material such as hadith. One of the most widely used and respected works of this type, is the Tafsir of Ismail Ibn Al-Kathir.

IqraSense.com

2. Understanding and Handling Life's Difficulties and Calamities

As part of our Islamic faith, we believe that all matters are in the hands of Allah. However, for some of us, our faith can get shaken during times of trials and hardships. But, it is precisely during those times that we should remind ourselves that a believer's position and rank are raised in front of Allah, and that such hardship may very well be a sign of Allah's love for the believer. This awareness, which comes through hardship, can help us to maintain, and even to strengthen our faith.

This chapter reviews the attitude that a Muslim needs to adopt to handle life's challenges and also steps that one can take to deal with them effectively.

2.1 A Muslim's Attitude Toward Challenges and Difficulties

We find guidance in Quran and Sunnah in adopting the right attitude to handle life's challenges and difficulties. Understanding this is a first step in handling those situations. Here are two reminders related to this.

Great Rewards are Associated with Great Calamities

It was narrated from Anas ibn Malik that the Prophet (S.A.W.S.) said:

"Great reward comes with great trials. When Allah loves a people, He tests them, and whoever accepts it attains His pleasure, whereas whoever shows discontent with it incurs His wrath."

Narrated and classed as hasan by at-Tirmidhi (2396); classed as saheeh by al-Albaani in as-Silsilah as-Saheehah, no. 146

In this hadith, we find that the Prophet (S.A.W.S.) provides a message of relief for those who endure difficulties with patience. He also associates the degree of the difficulties and calamities which the believer suffers, with higher rewards. So, enduring through lighter problems and challenges has a smaller reward than enduring greater difficulties and challenges. Given that this life has its share of challenges and difficulties for all, Allah has provided an opportunity of high rewards for those who endure these challenges with patience rather than with complaints and ingratitude. Further, those who show displeasure and discontent with Allah's decree end up in a lose-lose situation, because not only do they have to live through their current suffering, but they also incur Allah's wrath for their displeasure and discontent with His decree.

We should also realize that the patience which we show when facing difficulties raises our status in front of Allah, and may lead to the forgiveness of our sins. He says in the Quran:

"...Only those who are patient shall receive their reward in full, without reckoning" Quran (Surah Az-Zumar:10).

The Prophet (S.A.W.S.) said:

"Nothing befalls a believer, a (prick of a) thorn or more than that, but Allah will raise him one degree in status thereby, or erase a bad deed." Narrated by al-Bukhaari (5641) and Muslim (2573).

The Messenger (S.A.W.S.) said in a well-known hadith the following:

"How wonderful is the affair of the believer, for his affairs are all good, and this applies to no one but the believer. If something good happens to him, he is thankful for it and that is good for him. If something bad happens to him, he bears it with patience and that is good for him." (Narrated by Muslim, 2999).

We should also realize that when Allah puts His steadfast believers through trials and tribulations, that this is a sign of His love for them. It was narrated that Anas (may Allah be pleased with him) said:

"If Allah wills good for His slave, He hastens his punishment in this world, and if He wills bad for His slave, He withholds from him (the punishment for) his sin, until He requites him for it on the Day of Resurrection." Narrated and classed as hasan by at-Tirmidhi (2396); classed as saheeh by al-Albaani in Saheeh at-Tirmidhi.

Al-Hasan al-Basri (may Allah have mercy on him) said: "Do not resent the calamities that come and the disasters that occur, for perhaps in something that you dislike will be your salvation, and perhaps in something that you prefer will be your doom."

Al-Fadl ibn Sahl said: "There is a blessing in calamity that the wise man should not ignore, for it erases sins, gives one the opportunity to attain the reward for patience, dispels negligence, reminds one of blessings at the time of health, calls one to repent and encourages one to give charity."

Calamities and Problems – Trials or Punishment?

We also know that some who face difficulties are punished for their sins. So, one may wonder how to distinguish between a person who is simply being tested by Allah and one who is being punished for their sins. In this context, scholars have said that *"(as Allah knows a person beforehand), the sign of calamity by way of punishment shows as signs of impatience and ingratitude in a person when a calamity befalls, and the sign of calamity by way of expiation and erasing of sins shows as contentment, acceptance, and patience in accepting the will of Allah until relief comes."* Furthermore, if the one who is affected shows displeasure and panic, then it cannot be thought that his calamity is an honor from Allah to raise him in status, because Allah, may He be glorified, knew that he would not be patient and accept his difficulties with contentment. So in this case it is most likely that the hardship is a requital and punishment.

Also, if the Muslim is a devoted worshipper, obedient and righteous, and there is nothing between him and Allah but true 'uboodiyyah' (servitude), gratitude, praise, repentance and submission to Him, may He be glorified, then it is most likely that this calamity is a kind of honor and raising in status, and people are the witnesses of Allah on earth. If they know him to be righteous, then they may give him the glad tidings of raised status before Allah if he is patient in bearing the calamity. (source: islamqa.info)

Regarding difficulties, in the following verse Allah compares the situation of the one who is steadfast in his faith and facing difficulties with those who are evil doers and are in a similar situation:

"... if you are suffering (hardships) then surely, they (too) are suffering (hardships) as you are suffering, but you have a hope from Allah (for the reward) that for which they hope not; and Allah is Ever All-Knowing, All-Wise" Quran (Surah An-Nisa:104).

So, a true believer can face his difficulties with a positive state of mind, hoping for rewards from Allah. Such an attitude, in the face of hardships, can provide true relief and happiness. Besides, if Allah lifts this calamity from the believer and saves him from the torment, then that can double the reward and happiness. Allah says in the Quran:

- *"... and give glad tidings to As-Sabirun (the patient).*
- *Who, when afflicted with calamity, say: "Truly! To Allah we belong and truly, to Him we shall return."*
- *They are those on whom are the Salawat (i.e. who are blessed and will be forgiven) from their Lord, and (they are those who) receive His Mercy, and it is they who are the guided ones." Quran (Surah Al-Baqara:155-157)*

2.2 Dealing with Life's Challenges and Difficulties

As strategies for getting through life's problems are rarely formally learned, we are constrained to use trial and error which often results in suboptimal results. However, once learned, handling the difficulties in our lives can help us cope with them more effectively and move forward in life with a better mindset.

Dealing effectively with our difficulties and problems requires several strategies, appropriate emotional control, acceptance of realities, charting out a course of action, and finally taking preventive measures to keep future problems at bay. Thus, arming ourselves with the right intellectual, mental, and spiritual strategies to get through these phases can help us achieve successful breakthroughs, which allow us to overcome present hardships, and to learn how to more effectively counter them in the future.

Let us go over each of these steps in more detail.

The Emotional Response

An emotional response to a difficulty or calamity is both normal and only human. However, emotions have to be managed and channeled appropriately; if not, they can manifest negatively within our personalities and affect our lives in general. Research confirms that emotionally-reactive individuals, confronting even relatively minor challenges in their lives, become also prone to increased physical problems and diseases.

One way in which people channel their emotions is to act them out uncontrollably and irresponsibly. In such situations, the prophet

(S.A.W.S.) instructed us to exercise patience and to maintain a composed demeanor, instead of acting irresponsibly. When his son Ibrahim was dying, the prophet's eyes filled with tears. Abd al-Rahmaan ibn Awf said, *'Are you weeping when you have forbidden us to weep?'* **The Prophet said, *'I do not forbid weeping. What I have forbidden is two foolish and evil kinds of voices: voices at times of entertainment and play and the flutes of Shaytaan, and voices at times of calamity and scratching the face and rending the garments and screaming.'"*** [Al-Tirmidhi, al-Bayhaqi in al-Sunan al-Kubra (4/69), classed as hasan by al-Albaani]

In other cases, emotions are channeled inwardly to fester, which then leads to the development of a victimized mindset. You may not realize it, but believing that your life is a teary saga may be the anchor weighing you down and preventing you from moving forward in your life

So, be conscious of how you channel your emotions. You can temper them with positive thinking and a strong faith. If you show any signs of having a victimized mindset then you need to snap out of it and adopt a more positive and reality based mindset instead. That can put you on the right path to get out of your difficulties faster.

Trying To Make Sense Of The Difficulties

The divine decree: When facing difficulties, our weak faith can sometimes drive us to question the fairness of it all. In this context, we should remind ourselves that believing in Al-Qadr (Allah's divine will and decree) is one of the pillars of Islamic faith. As the Prophet (S.A.W.S.) said, it means belief in (1) Allah, (2) Angels, (3) revealed Holy Books (Quran, Bible, Torah, etc.), (4) His Messengers, (5) Day of Judgment, and (6) to believe in al-qadar (the divine decree) both good and bad. Allah also says in the Quran, **"No calamity befalls on the earth or in your selves but it is inscribed in the book of decrees (al-lawh al-Mahfooz) before we bring it into existence. Verily, that is easy for Allah." Quran (Surah Al-hadeed:22).**

As part of that belief, we should recognize that Allah does what He wills for reasons that are known only to Him. Any attempt to comprehend His wisdom with our limited minds, or to understand how our current situation fits in His overall plan, can lead us only to erroneous conclusions.

The "If-Only" Trap: Another trap that many of us fall into has to do with using the "if-only" logic. Very often, our minds tell us that "if I could have done such and such, then this wouldn't have happened." The prophet (S.A.W.S.) warned us against falling into such satanic traps. In a hadith narrated by Abu Hurayrah, the prophet remarked,

"…If anything befalls you, do not say 'If only I had done (such and such), the such and such would have happened,' rather say: 'Allah has decreed and what He wills He does,' for 'if only' opens the door to the work of the shaytaan." Narrated by Muslim (2664).

We see another example of this during the battle of Uhud when many Muslims died. This gave the hypocrites an excuse to criticize the divine decree. But Allah refuted their claims by stating (interpretation of the meaning): ***"Say: 'Even if you had remained in your homes, those for whom death was decreed would certainly have gone forth to the place of their death'".*** Quran (Surah Aal-e-Imraan:154).

This further goes to show that what Allah decrees is inevitable. Any attempt to imagine a different outcome based on different actions that we could have taken in the past will only increase our frustrations. This belief is also a blessing, because it prevents us from returning to the past that can result in nothing but an added emotional baggage.

In this context, many among us also resort to blaming people, including those close to us. This blaming attitude in turn nurtures a mindset where people (even within families) resist future temptations to recommend anything or engage in an open dialogue. This not only weakens communications amongst people but also causes irreparable rifts and a loss of trust between them.

To summarize, accepting the divine decree can help us in not only forgoing the past but to also win Allah's pleasure. Suppressing our urge to blame others by maintaining a positive mindset can help us maintain healthy relationships and in keeping good advice flowing from others.

Getting Yourself Out Of Trouble

Having accepted Allah's decree, and after getting over any emotional challenges, the next step involves taking the right actions to get us out of our problems and difficulties. Actively engaging our God gifted faculties to pull us out of such situations is not as common as one may think. Thus, many a time we fail to achieve successful breakthroughs because we either follow a haphazard approach to resolve our problems or give up on our efforts too early in the process. This leads us to get stalled and makes us regard situations as irresolvable, resulting in our hoping and praying for miracles to pull us out.

If you find yourself in such situations, this may be the time to rethink your overall approach. You see, most of us are accustomed to looking for "silver bullet" types of solutions. However, such solutions are not that common and thus can't be relied on to get you out of your life's challenges. Adopting a realistic but methodical approach instead has a better chance of bringing you closer to your desired outcomes.

This requires that you take time to define the problems and difficulties that you face with increased clarity and specificity. This is bound to yield better results because you will get clearer about the outcomes that you desire. You will also be able to clearly delineate the constituent tasks that potentially can put you closer to your desired solution. Follow those tasks through to the end with perseverance and patience and you may reduce the load of your problems.

On the spiritual front, we should recognize that if Allah puts us through trials or punishes us because of our sins, the decision is His. However, seeking forgiveness through repentance (Istighfar) can help undo the damage of our sins. As the prophet (S.A.W.S.) said: *"whoever does a lot of Istighfar, Allah will provide him a way out of each concern he has, and will solve all his troubles, and will provide him with livelihood from sources that were not known to him" (Narrated by Imam Ahmad, Sanad Saheeh.)*

Preventive measures

Finally, although Allah's decree is ordained, there are things we can do beforehand to influence the outcome of our efforts, and thus prevent problems from piling up. First, we should never forget that Allah has provided us with a free will and associated faculties to think and act. As the prophet had stated, while we should fully trust Allah, we should tie our horse first – meaning we should use all our God-gifted faculties and exercise the required due diligence.

Second, for cases in which we fumble to choose between options, we should exercise the use of the 'Istikhara' prayers. The text of the Du'a recited in those prayers clearly reflects your plea to Allah to make the desired decision work for you if it's good for you, or to ward it off if it's not. By doing so, you consciously put your faith in Him to guide you. This will reduce the likelihood of you ending up with a failed outcome and thus an added burden for you to carry in the future.

Conclusion

To summarize, remember that effectively channeling your emotions, letting go of a negative past, maximizing the use of your God-gifted faculties, and above all maintaining a strong faith can help you attain the wisdom that life demands from you to get through even the most difficult challenges. Just ensure that you get serious about resisting the old habits and inculcate a positive mindset to propel you forward.

— End

3. Keeping a Strong Faith during Tough Times

As we go through hardships and calamities, it is natural to get swept away by the affliction of the moment. During such trials of faith, unless we are careful, Satan can inject fear and plant doubts into our hearts and minds. Our beliefs in such vulnerable states may become overpowered by feelings of the moment, resulting in the dwindling of our faith. Some of us start questioning the fairness and wisdom underlying such divine decisions while others get mired in a blame game. All in all, we may find ourselves lost, helpless, and stalled, making it difficult to gather ourselves and move forward.

For such situations, Islamic teachings guide us to stay in control by hanging on to the Mercy and Grace of Allah. We pray that Allah keeps us safe from the challenges and trials of life, but as Muslims we should all know and understand Quran's message and the prophet's guidance for handling tough moments in life. The following paragraphs summarize some of the key guidance regarding this matter.

3.1 Do Not Feel Helpless

Even when all doors appear to have been closed, as true believers we should never allow ourselves to succumb to feelings of helplessness.

Consider the following hadith of the prophet (S.A.W.S.) and ibn Al-Qayyim's commentary on that hadith:

It was narrated from Abu Hurayrah (may Allah be pleased with him) that the Prophet (peace and blessings of Allah be upon him) said: "The strong believer is better and more beloved to Allah than the weak believer, although both are good. Strive to do that which will benefit you and seek the help of Allah, and do not feel helpless. If anything befalls you, do not say 'If only I had done (such and such), the such and such would have happened,' rather say: 'Allah has decreed and what He wills He does,' for 'if only' opens the door to the work of the shaytaan." Narrated by Muslim (2664).

Ibn al-Qayyim (may Allah have mercy on him) said: "*This hadeeth includes several important principles of faith, including the following:*

Then he said: "and do not feel helpless", because feeling helpless is contrary to striving for that which will benefit him, and it is contrary to seeking the help of Allah. The one who strives for that which will benefit him and seeks the help of Allah is the opposite of the one who feels helpless, so this is telling him, before what has been decreed happens, of that which is one of the greatest means of attaining it, which is striving for it whilst seeking the help of the One in Whose hand is control of all things, from Whom they come and to Whom they will return. If he does not attain what was not decreed for him, then he may feel either of two things: helplessness, which opens the door to the work of the shaytaan, so his sense of helplessness leads him to say "if only", but there is nothing good in saying "if only" in this case, rather that opens the door to blame, panic, discontentment, regret and grief, all of which are the work of the shaytaan. So, the Prophet (peace and blessings of Allah be upon him) forbade us to open the door to his works in this manner, and told us to adopt the second option, which is looking at the divine decree and bearing it in mind, for if it was decreed for him it would never have missed him and no one could have prevented him from attaining it. Hence he said: "If anything befalls you, do not say 'If only I had done (such and such), the such and such would have happened,' rather say: 'Allah has decreed and what He wills He does,'" and he taught him that which will benefit him in either case, whether he gets what he wanted or not. Hence this hadeeth is one which a person can never do without. [Source: Shifa' al-'Aleel (37-38).]

3.2 Revive Your Faith

As mentioned in the hadith above, a strong faith can help us to hold our heads high. When faith seems to be dwindling, we should get back to Quran and remind ourselves that only Allah can let us out of our ordeal and our problems. You must, therefore, keep that faith and not let Satan instill thoughts in your heart and mind that could weaken your faith. Allah says in the Quran:

"If Allah helps you, none can overcome you; and if He forsakes you, who is there after Him that can help you? And in Allah (Alone) let believers put their trust." Quran (Surah Aal-e-Imran:160)

A strong faith can keep you focused on the fact that Allah alone ultimately controls all destinies and has power over all things. Simply remembering that fact at the moment of affliction can help you in conquering the pain and can provide you the hope and the energy that you need to keep moving forward.

3.3 Believe in the Divine Decree

When facing difficulties, our weak faith can sometimes drive us to question the fairness of what befalls us in terms of hardships. In this context, we should remind ourselves that believing in *al-Qadr* (Allah's divine will and decree) is one of the pillars of Islamic faith. As we know, the pillars of the Islamic faith are belief in (1) Allah, (2) His Angels, (3) His revealed Holy Books (Quran, Bible, Torah, Zabur), (4) His Messengers, (5) Day of Judgment, and (6) to believe in al-Qadar (the divine decree), both good and bad. Allah also says in the Quran:

- **No calamity befalls on the earth or in yourselves but is inscribed in the Book of Decrees (Al-Lauh Al-Mahfooz), before We bring it into existence. Verily, that is easy for Allah.**
- **In order that you may not grieve at the things that you fail to get, nor rejoice over that which has been given to you. And Allah likes not prideful boasters.**

  Quran (Surah Al-Hadid:22-23)

As part of that belief, we should, therefore, recognize that Allah does what He wills for reasons that are known only to Him. Any attempt to comprehend the wisdom of it all using our limited faculties, or to understand how our current situation fits in His overall plan can only lead us to erroneous conclusions, which will only increase our frustration. We, as Muslims, should accept Allah's Decree both as it manifests itself around us and in our lives. It should be a relief to us that Allah alone is the master of our destiny and we are going to be tested on our ability to be patient in adversity and grateful in prosperity.

3.4 Ask for Allah's Mercy for an Out from Tough Situations

As believers we should recognize that only Allah's Grace and Mercy can deliver us from challenging situations. Allah tells us in the Quran:

"Then after that you turned away. Had it not been for the Grace and Mercy of Allah upon you, indeed you would have been among the losers." Quran (Surah Al-Baqara:64)

Another way to ask for Allah's Grace and Mercy is by asking for His forgiveness and seeking repentance. Allah tells us in the Quran:

'And (commanding you): "Seek the forgiveness of your Lord, and turn to Him in repentance, that He may grant you good enjoyment, for a term appointed, and bestow His abounding Grace to every owner of grace (i.e. the one who helps and serves needy and

deserving, physically and with his wealth, and even with good words). But if you turn away, then I fear for you the torment of a Great Day (i.e. the Day of Resurrection).' Quran (Surah Al-Hud:3).

3.5 Stay Patient in Hard Times

One of the best remedies for tough times is to be patient. A state of patience requires that we not resort to complaining, and remember Allah often. We take this lesson from the story of Prophet Yousuf (A.S.) who went through various ordeals in life only to be rewarded with a large kingdom in his later years. Allah tells us in the Quran:

They said: "Are you indeed Yousuf (Joseph)?" He said: "I am Yousuf (Joseph), and this is my brother (Benjamin). Allah has indeed been gracious to us. Verily, he who fears Allah with obedience to Him (by abstaining from sins and evil deeds, and by performing righteous good deeds), and is patient, then surely, Allah makes not the reward of the Muhsinoon (good-doers) to be lost." Quran (Surah Yousuf:90).

The Quran also says:

"Thus did We give full authority to Yousuf (Joseph) in the land, to take possession therein, as when or where he likes. We bestow of Our Mercy on whom We please, and We make not to be lost the reward of Al-Muhsinoon (the good doers)." Quran (Surah Yousuf:56).

3.6 Remember Allah in Good Times

We know from the Quran that when we remember Allah in good times, Allah will help us in tough times. We learn from the story of Prophet Younus (A.S.) that when he was swallowed by a whale, Allah relieved him of his torment because of his remembrance of Allah. He tells us in the Quran:

- *Had he not been of them who glorify Allah,*
- *He would have indeed remained inside its belly (the fish) till the Day of Resurrection.*

Quran (Surah As-Saaffaat:143, 144)

To summarize, the next time when you are in a tough situation that may potentially test your will and faith, remember these points:

1. Do not let yourself get to a point where you feel helpless.
2. Revive your faith by reciting Quran and ponder over Allah's words.
3. Recall your faith in the Divine Decree.
4. Ask for Allah's Mercy and Grace for an Out from Tough Situations (by making all the Du'a that the Prophet (S.A.W.S.) taught us).
5. Remember Allah in good times.

6. Stay patient until Allah guides you out from the tough situation you are in.

Finally, let us not forget what Allah told us the following in the Quran:

"Say: 'Nothing shall ever happen to us except what Allah has ordained for us. He is our Maula (Lord, Helper and Protector).' And in Allah let the believers put their trust" Quran (Surah Towbah:51).

– End

4. Matters of the (Muslim) Heart

In a metaphysical, metaphorical, and in a very literal sense, we use our hearts in a variety of interesting ways, in every aspect of our lives. We love, hate, shed tears, feel happy, etc. all based on the beliefs and understanding of various matters that we hold in our hearts. In a very real way, our behavior is largely driven by the world that we build in our hearts. People are known to go to great lengths to perform acts that range from being heroic to being absurd, all based on the value that one places on various matters, whether they be people and things, in one's heart.

It is no wonder then that Allah mentions the "heart", in various contexts, in over 100 places throughout the Quran.

Consider, for example, what the prophet said in a hadith:

"There is a piece of flesh in the body if it becomes good (reformed) the whole body becomes good but if it gets spoiled, the whole body gets spoiled – and that is the heart." [Bukhary, Volume 1, Book 2, Number 49: Part of the Hadith Narrated by An-Nu'man bin Bashir]

If what we hold in our hearts drives us to act – sometimes pushing us to extremes – then it's only prudent that we feed the right beliefs and knowledge to the world of our hearts.

Without proper knowledge and religious understanding, we can't expect to build the levels of our faith, and without faith there can't be devotion in our actions. Ibn Al-Qayyim said, *"..if actions were useful without devotion, He (Allah) would never have dispraised the hypocrites."* He also said, *"Allah will never purchase any good (deed) that has not been refined by faith."* (Al Fawwaid)

It should come as no surprise therefore that we will be questioned about the knowledge that we acquire and about the ways in which we use knowledge to build the worlds of our hearts.

Consider the following verse:

"…and follow not (o man, i.e., say not, or do not, or witness not) that of which you have no knowledge. Verily, the hearing, and the sight, and the heart of each of those ones will be questioned (by Allah)" Quran (Surah Al-Israa:36)

We know that the foundation of our religious understanding is based on our upbringing and our continued efforts to acquire knowledge. The weaker the foundation, the more difficult it becomes to live Islam. A weak foundation also lets a carefree attitude take root in our hearts, making us even more negligent of our priorities. One of the pious and knowledgeable salaf 'Ata' al-Sulaymi was asked about his fear of Allah and his concerns and he said: *"…. death is close at hand, the grave is my house, on the day of resurrection I will stand and my path is over a bridge across hell, and i do not know what will become of me."*

Obviously, if our knowledge and understanding are weak, our minds wouldn't worry about such matters.

Unfortunately, in such a state many people don't even want to be aware of their ignorance, of the things that they don't know, and the things which they need to know.

In distinction to this, when we invest in building the foundations of our knowledge and religious understanding, we become more cognizant of Allah and fear Him accordingly.

For those of us who feel better about their levels of knowledge, understanding and faith, we need to be mindful and to ensure that we do not develop a false sense of 'Iman' (faith). This is because we live in a world where it is common to find religious understanding founded on superficial knowledge garbled with philosophies of the day (that abound) and bits of personal viewpoints.

Sometimes that religious understanding is also tainted with cultural norms, giving rise to Islamic viewpoints that are not in line with what was revealed by Allah on our prophet Muhammad (S.A.W.S.).

We, therefore, should be wary of falling into such traps of distorted enlightenment.

Consider the example of Umar Al-Khattab (the second Caliph of Islam). ***The prophet had said that if there was going to be a prophet after him, it would have been Umar.*** It was the same Umar who on his deathbed asked for his head to be put on sand and he kept saying that *"...may God be merciful on me. Oh you whose kingship never deviates have mercy on the one whose kingship has just deviated."*

If even Umar – one of the very few who had been promised paradise in his life – was so worried and anxious about getting Allah's mercy, how can we become complacent about the levels of the faith and 'Iman' that live in our hearts?

Elevating our knowledge and religious understanding thus should be given a renewed sense of urgency. Let us remind ourselves that the excuses that we may have today for not enhancing or correcting our religious knowledge and understanding, won't pass the test of time: they have not for anyone in the past.

Ibn Al-Qayyim said, *"the person who is profoundly knowledgeable of Allah would be interested in consolidating the foundation and strengthening it. And the ignorant person would be interested in constructing but without taking care of the foundation, and in no time, his establishment would collapse."*

Allah says in the Quran:

> **"Is it then he, who laid the foundation of his building on piety to Allah and his good pleasure, better, or he who laid the foundation of his building on an undetermined brink of a precipice (steep rock) ready to crumble down, so that it crumbled to pieces with him into the fire of hell?" (At-Tawbah, 9:109)**

Getting the right knowledge will also elevate our positions in front of our Creator. As Allah says:

"Allah will exalt in degree those of you who believe, and those who have been granted knowledge" Quran (Surah Al-Mujaadilah:11)

Finally, a useful Du'a that we can make to inculcate the fear of our Creator is the one taught to us by the prophet. He (S.A.W.S.) used to make the dua:

"I seek refuge in you, O Allah!, from knowledge that does not benefit and from a heart which does not fear."

Let us therefore spend our time to acquire the knowledge that can correct the condition of our hearts and make our lives a bit more meaningful. Let us also be wary of what we are not feeding our hearts. Ultimately, we are revealed to people, and revealed to our Creator, based on what's in our hearts.

-- End

5. Taking Stock of our "Thinking" Abilities

Allah, when explaining the message revealed in Quran, repeatedly challenges mankind to "think" and "think deeply". One wonders how this is different from the "regular thinking" that we engage in on a day-to-day basis. Our thinking processes enable us to reach conclusions, make decisions, and solve problems constantly. However, a detailed study of the Quran reveals that these terms allude to a more rigorous form of thinking, which in today's terms can be equated with "critical thinking".

The difference between the two forms of thinking – regular thinking and critical thinking – is quite profound. For the purpose of our understanding, let us consider one of the definitions provided by *The Foundation for Critical Thinking*: *"Critical thinking is that mode of thinking – about any subject, content, or problem – in which the thinker improves the quality of his or her thinking by skillfully taking charge of the structures inherent in thinking and imposing intellectual standards upon them."* It further states that *"critical thinking is self-guided, self-disciplined thinking which attempts to reason at the highest level of quality in a fair-minded way."*

Quran advocates this level of "thinking" because, naturally, superficial thinking alone isn't enough to cut through the beliefs and faiths that people have held onto for centuries. As "thinking deeply" allows people to question their internal biases and notice patterns that otherwise they may not be able to see, such thinking has allowed many over hundreds of years to understand Quran's divine message, and, accordingly, to reconstruct their belief patterns and come into the fold of Islam.

Quranic verses expand on this form of "thinking" throughout, by asking mankind to *observe, seek knowledge, reflect,* and *ask questions* and to ultimately connect the dots by *using the faculties of human reason.* Other similar terms used in the Quran in various contexts can best be translated as "to reason", "reflect", "ponder", etc. Understandably so, a cursory and superficial study of the Quran (e.g. merely relying on translations) carries the risk of the divine message being misunderstood and misrepresented, something that unfortunately seems to be quite common today.

The following are some of the examples (parts of verses) where Allah has mentioned the use of reason and thinking in various contexts.

- *Verily, in this is indeed a sign <u>for people who think</u>. Quran (Surah An-Nahl:69)*
- *Do they not <u>think deeply</u> (in their own selves) about themselves (how Allah created them from nothing, and similarly He will resurrect them)?....... Quran (Surah Ar-room:8)*
- *.... so that their hearts (and minds) may <u>thus use reason</u>... Quran (Surah Al-Hajj:46)*
- *...in all this] there are messages/signs indeed for people who <u>use their reason</u>. Quran (Surah Al-Baqarah:164)*
- *Those who remember Allah (always, and in prayers) standing, sitting, and lying down on their sides, and <u>think</u>*

deeply about the creation of the heavens and the earth….. Quran (Suran Aal-e-Imran:191)
- ……….. So relate the stories, _perhaps they may reflect_. Quran (Surah Al-A'raaf:176)
- _Do they not reflect_? There is no madness in their companion (Muhammad). He is but a plain warner. Quran (Surah Al-A'raaf:184)
- …. Such are the parables which We put forward to mankind that _they may reflect_. Quran (Surah Al-Hashr:21)

It is well known that critical thinking skills have to be learned. There is also abundant research which supports the contention that learning in today's world is mostly information-oriented and based on providing ready-made answers rather than challenging people to think creatively and critically, which would help them understand issues better, decide intelligently, and resolve problems. Even in a technologically advanced country such as the US, a study (documented in a book called Academically Adrift: Limited Learning on College Campuses) shows that a relatively high percentage of students demonstrated no significant improvement in their critical thinking and reasoning skills as they graduated and entered adult life.

Sadly enough, a considerable percentage of us probably fall into that category as well.

When you are not thinking critically, your understanding of the issues is usually muddled and vague. You are more prone to jump to conclusions based on limited information. Your decisions cannot be expected to be sound, because you haven't taken the time to consider alternatives and compare options. You are driven more by various biases and emotions, rather than being open minded and listening with an attentive ear. Unfortunately, such thinking habits can lead you to make the wrong decisions (or no decisions at all) and sap away your problem solving abilities, thus increasing your life's inventory of problems.

On the contrary, thinking critically can bring order to your thinking processes. When you force yourself to *define the issues and problems clearly*, you can select better approaches to resolve them. *Gaining more knowledge* can help you get a better view of the landscape that you are facing. *Asking the right questions* can help you disentangle from the problems faster. *Generating alternatives* and *comparing options* push you forward toward resolution of your problems. *Applying sound logic and reason* helps in bridging the gaps in your thinking. All in all, *taking the needed time* to go through the rigors of "thinking" can help you draw warranted conclusions, render accurate judgments and arrive at sound decisions.

Even if you don't find solutions to your issues, you would have at least maximized your mind power to contribute toward your well-being.

Finally, let us not forget that if Allah challenged the non-believers to employ the faculties of human reason and thinking to help them get over their beliefs they have held for centuries – something that is not just sacrosanct but also one of the most difficult things to overcome –

we too, then, can use those mental faculties to get over any of the problems that we face in our daily lives.

-- End

6. Aligning Our Time to Life's Purpose

Are we making the best use of our time in this life? Are we to simply pass our time in whatever way possible so that we can get to the hereafter? How are we to balance our time across various aspects of this life? Is there a right balance? Are our life's priorities purpose driven?

These are some of the questions we Muslims ought to ask ourselves in order to get the most from our lives. It matters because we have at best only a few years to live. Considering the various phases of our lives individually, the available time is even shorter. Have you thought whether you will be satisfied when you get to the end of the road? Would you do things differently if you knew how much time you had left? What if your remaining time is very little?

Time is passing us quickly – and as it does, we should ask ourselves whether we have much to show for it. Are we fulfilling both our religious and worldly responsibilities? Are our families getting their fair share or is it all about other matters? Are we balancing our time across all other obligations? Are we even conscious about how we use our time?

Time is therefore one of the most valuable assets that we have. Being wise in the use of that asset is thus only prudent. Time is one of the many things that Allah has used to swear by in the Quran (verse 1 of Surah Al-Asr). The Prophet (S.A.W.S.), too, told us to use time to make the most of certain assets before time takes it away from us. He (peace and blessings of Allah be upon him) said:

"Make the most of five things before five others: <u>LIFE</u> before death, <u>HEALTH</u> before sickness, <u>FREE TIME</u> before becoming busy, <u>YOUTH</u> before old age, and <u>WEALTH</u> before poverty."
[Saheeh al-Jaami', no. 1077.]

Those who have run out of time will tell us its value. Ask the old who have nearly run out of time or ask the terminally ill who have been given only a few months to live. They will tell us how productive they would be if they were given more time.

The reality is that our lives are too busy and our daily routines too engaging to allow us to pause and assess what we are earning, or what opportunities we may be missing as we pass our allotted time. But here are some of the things we can do to ensure that we use our remaining time in this life effectively.

6.1 Be Mindful Of Your Purpose In This Life

As Muslims, we believe that Allah not only created mankind but clarified their purpose of being here. That may seem quite obvious to some but questions related to the "purpose and meaning of life" have been grappled with even by western and non-Muslim philosophers for centuries. The foundation of our Islamic beliefs encourages us to not get entangled in the philosophical innuendos of the topic. Islamic principles make it clear that Allah created life, this universe, and the rules that embody it. And mankind is to worship Him by submitting to those rules.

Amongst the many, consider the following three verses –

"And I (Allah) created not the jinn and mankind except that they should worship Me (Alone)" Quran (Surah adh-Dhaariyaat:56).

"Say (O Muhammad): Verily, my Salaah (prayer), my sacrifice, my living, and my dying are for Allah, the Lord of the 'Aalameen (mankind, jinn and all that exists)" Quran (Surah al-An'aam:162)

"Did you think that We had created you in play (without any purpose), and that you would not be brought back to Us?" Quran (Surah al-Mu'minoon:115)

It is perhaps needless to explain, but a sense of purpose can help in reconciling the many complex questions and issues that are not always that easy for us to comprehend. Purpose helps in instilling the energy that we need to keep moving forward, irrespective of the challenges that we face, and to adhere to a system of living that we believe was designed by the Creator for His Creation.

6.2 Become More Action Oriented

As straightforward as it may seem, there is something inherently complex about taking action in life that leads to many failing to accomplish enough. Ask yourself if you could have accomplished more by this time in your life by taking more actions in the past? What is it that stopped you from accomplishing more? As it turns out, many of us fall victim to procrastination, never ending planning, or simply failing to have the discipline or courage to decide to act at the right time. The result is that time passes without us accomplishing much, or, at least not as much as we could have.

As Muslims, we will be judged on what we do. Our faith is incomplete without us following up on it through actions. There are many places in the Quran where the mention of faith is coupled with the need to take action. Consider these verses from Quran:

- *By Al-Asr (the time).*
- *Verily! Man is in loss,*
- *Except those who believe (in Islamic Monotheism) and do righteous good deeds, and recommend one another to the truth (i.e. order one another to perform all kinds of good deeds which Allah has ordained, and abstain from all kinds of sins and evil deeds which Allah has forbidden), and recommend one another to patience.*

    Quran (Surah Al-Asr)

In another place in the Quran, Allah warns us about putting our words into practice. He says in the Quran,

"O you who believe! Why do you say that which you do not do? Most hateful it is with Allah that you say that which you do not do" Quran (Surah As-Saff:2-3)

By refocusing, and becoming more action oriented, we can accomplish more and thus make our life more fulfilling.

6.3 Don't Concern Yourself With Unnecessary Matters

Today, we find ourselves exposed to a wide range of information outlets waiting to distract us from key priorities. Between the Internet, satellite TV and various forms of staying connected, we can end up wasting useful time soaking our minds with information that we usually can do without. While a lot of such information may satiate our curiosities and gossipy habits, they take up valuable time and drain our energies – both of which can instead be used to gain the right knowledge, fulfill our responsibilities, and in taking useful actions. Remember what the prophet said:

"From the perfection of a person's Islam is that he leaves alone that which does not concern him." (Reported From Abu Hurairah – Tirmidhee (no. 2318) and others).

So, as various media channels provide us with the opportunity to get plugged in to a world of information and knowledge, we must become selective in its use based on what benefits us.

6.4 Don't Forget The Daily Remembrance Of Allah

Many of us make the mistake of taking advice about remembering Allah as merely a spiritual matter, and of having no connection with the real, practical world. Instead, we should remind ourselves that our success in this life (related to our work, earnings, family, health, etc.) is tied to the remembrance of Allah (in prayers and at other times as well during the day). Consider what Allah tells us in the Quran:

"...and seek the Bounty of Allah, and remember Allah much, that you may be successful" Quran (Surah al-Jumu'ah:10)

In another verse, He says:

"O you who believe! Let not your properties or your children divert you from the remembrance of Allah. And whosoever does that, then they are the losers." Quran (Surah Al-Munafiqoon:9)

The Prophet Muhammad (S.A.W.S.) also said:

"Should I not inform you of the best of deeds, and the most sanctifying of deeds before your Lord, which does more to raise your positions (with Him), and is better for you than the

disbursement of gold and money, or battle with the enemy?" They (the companions) said: "Indeed inform us." He (S.A.W.S.) then said: "Remembrance of Allah." [Narrated by At-Tirmidhi, 5/459; Ibn Maajah, 2/1245]

Taking the time to pause often and to reassess how we use our time can help us refocus, reprioritize and reenergize. It can also prevent us from going to extremes, where we focus on certain priorities of life more than others. Applying these principles in our actions and accomplishments can help us get the most of our time.

-- End

7. The Blessings of Gratitude and Shukr

Gratitude (shukr) is about expressing thanks and appreciation to those who do any favor to us. Obviously, none can come close to our creator, Allah, who gave us everything. As the Quran states: **"Who created you, fashioned you perfectly, and gave you due proportion" Quran (Surah Al-Infitar:7).** As humans, Allah has bestowed on us the nature to be grateful and we should thus express that gratitude not just to Allah but to the people whom we deal with as well. In many places in the Quran, Allah divides people as being grateful and as ungrateful to motivate us to join the camp of those who are grateful. In one of such verses, Prophet Sulaiman said, as stated in the Quran, **"... then when (Sulaiman (Solomon)) saw it placed before him, he said: "This is by the Grace of my Lord to test me whether I am grateful or ungrateful! And whoever is grateful, truly, his gratitude is for (the good of) his own self, and whoever is ungrateful, (he is ungrateful only for the loss of his own self). Certainly! My Lord is Rich (Free of all wants), Bountiful", Quran (Surah An-Naml:40).**

Having a sense of gratitude is thus a great blessing, and those of us who instill that sense within ourselves not only seek Allah's pleasure but also embody a sense of happiness, relieving us of the many pressures and anxieties of life. Although the blessings and benefits of gratitude are many, this chapter highlights certain important ones that you should recognize and use as a means to motivate that sense within yourselves.

Gratitude is knowing that whatever we have is from Allah. Gratitude helps us focus our minds on Allah, something that has unfortunately become so difficult today on account of life's distractions and attractions. Gratitude, therefore, corrects our perceptions by reminding us that everything that happens to us doesn't happen because of its own volition and thus we should not take matters for "granted". Allah says in the Quran: *"And whatever of blessings and good things you have, it is from Allah" Quran (Surah al-Nahl:53).* He also says, *"And He found you poor and made you rich (self-sufficient with self-contentment)" Quran (Surah ad-Duha:8).* Let us therefore constantly remind ourselves of Allah's bounties by expressing our gratitude to Him in prayers and at other times.

Gratitude helps in warding off punishment from Allah. Not recognizing Allah's blessings can keep us from gaining His pleasure. We know that if Allah were to punish us for our negligence, He would be justified for it. He says in the Quran: *"If Allah took mankind to task by that which they deserve, He would not leave a living creature on the surface of the earth; but He grants them reprieve unto an appointed term, and when their term comes – then verily Allah is Ever All-Seer of His slaves" Quran (Surah Fatir:45).* At the same time though, Allah provides us a way to escape that punishment by being thankful to Him. He says, *"Why should Allah punish you if you have thanked (Him) and have believed in Him. And Allah is Ever All-Appreciative (of good), All-Knowing" Quran (Surah An-Nisa: 147).* Gratitude, therefore, is not an option and we should clean our hearts to thank Allah for everything that He has provided us.

Gratitude helps us to slow down and to enjoy what we have rather than always waiting for the next wish to come true. Gratitude can help us recognize that we already have enough of what many people have for long been yearning for. We must therefore tame our *'Nafs'* (self) to understand that if we can't find happiness in the blessings that we have today, then we won't be happy with what we get tomorrow. Gratitude is a sense of fulfillment that comes not from wanting more but rather from a sense of knowing that Allah has already blessed us with what we need. In one of the hadiths the Prophet (S.A.W.S.) said: **"…if the son of Adam has one valley, he will wish that he had a second, and if he had two valleys, he would wish that he had a third. The stomach of the son of Adam will be filled only with dust (i.e., he is never satisfied)…" (Reported by Ahmad, 5/219; Saheeh Al-Jaami', 1781).** So, let us use gratitude to learn to enjoy what we have rather than fretting over what we don't.

Gratitude sought by exercising patience against unlawful desires prevents us from harmful consequences later. This was very aptly addressed by Ibn Qayyim, who stated that *"Patience in resisting desires is easier than patience in dealing with the consequences that result from going along with desires, because it either leads to pain and punishment or it prevents a more complete pleasure,…or it deprives one of a blessing, having which is more pleasurable and better than fulfilling desires,… or it cuts off an oncoming blessing, or it has a negative impact on one's character that will remain, because deeds have a great impact on one's character and behavior."* [Al-Fawaa'id (p. 139)]

Gratitude trains our minds to focus on the right things in life. It's akin to walking in a room filled with various colored items and focusing only on items of a specific color. If you do so, your mind will be able to easily mask the other colors as you focus on items of that specific color. Our life is no different. When we let our minds look for problems, we see plenty of them. Instead, if we rather look away from problems and focus on possibilities and go for solutions, we will get those too. Let us, therefore, use gratitude to motivate ourselves to find possibilities and solutions and not the negatives associated with problems.

Gratitude helps us recognize other people's favors on us. The Prophet (S.A.W.S.) through his sayings made it quite clear that expressing our gratitude to Allah by thanking Him also involves that we thank people who do favors for us. Prophet Muhammad (S.A.W.S.) said as narrated by Abu Hurairah: *"He who does not thank people, does not thank Allah" (Ahmad, Tirmidhi).* He also said: *"Whoever does you a favor, then reciprocate, and if you cannot find anything with which to reciprocate, then pray for him until you think that you have reciprocated him" Abu Dawood (1672).* In another hadith, he said: *"Whoever has a favor done for him and says to the one who did it, 'Jazak Allahu khayran,' (May Allah reward you) has done enough to thank him"* [Classed as saheeh by al-Albaani in Saheeh al-Tirmidhi]. Let us therefore ensure that we do our part to sincerely thank our families and those who have done good to us.

Gratitude isn't about ignoring our problems. On the contrary, gratitude helps us to be patient, accepting of life's trials, and accordingly trains us to seek personal fulfillment with less. Gratitude thus makes us "low maintenance" in our demands and expectations. This trait reduces our burden on those around us, making our company more pleasing to others instead of leaving us always unhappy, more demanding, and impossible to please because of unending requirements.

Gratitude is going beyond words and instead thanking through our actions. We see this in the example of the prophet whose sins were forgiven by Allah although he continued to strive for His pleasure. It was narrated that Aa'ishah said: *"When the Messenger of Allah (S.A.W.S.) prayed, he would stand for so long that his feet would become swollen. 'Aa'ishah said: O Messenger of Allah, are you doing this when Allah has forgiven your past and future sins? He said: "O 'Aa'ishah, should I not be a thankful slave?"* Narrated by al-Bukhaari (4557) and Muslim (2820). Let us, therefore, pray the extra 'nawafil' as one way to thank Allah for His blessings.

Gratitude helps increase one's blessings. Allah says: *"And (remember) when your Lord proclaimed: 'If you give thanks (by accepting Faith and worshipping none but Allah), I will give you more (of My Blessings); but if you are thankless, verily, My punishment is indeed severe'" Quran (Surah Ibraaheem:7)* Let us, therefore, make thanking Allah part of morning and evening remembrances (adhkars) to get more of Allah's blessings in our lives.

Gratitude helps us to get the pleasure of Allah in the hereafter. This is especially true when in Paradise we express our gratitude to Allah for His blessings to enter us into paradise. Abul-Abbaas al-Qurtubi said: *"... gratitude for blessings – even if they are few – is a means of attaining the pleasure of Allah, may He be exalted, which is the noblest situation of the people of Paradise. When the people of Paradise say, "You*

(Allah) have given to us what You have not given to anyone among Your creation," Allah will say to them: "Shall I not give you something better than that?" They will say, "What is it? Have You not brightened our faces, and admitted us to Paradise and saved us from Hell?" Allah will say, **"I bestow My pleasure upon you, and I will never be angry with you after that."** [Al-Mufhim lima ashkala min Talkhees Kitaab Muslim (7/60, 61)].

What better reward can we expect? So, why not be grateful to Him for what He has provided us day and night?

Finally, gratitude's importance was emphasized by the Prophet when he took the hand of Mu'aadh ibn Jabal and said: *"O Mu'aadh, by Allah I love you, by Allah I love you."* Then he said, *"I advise you, O Mu'aadh, do not fail to say this after every prayer: O Allah help me to remember You, to thank You and to worship You properly."* [Sahih Ahmad 5:245, Sahih abu Dawud 2:86, an-Nasa'i]

The Arabic version of this du'aa Hadith is the following. Let us ensure that we memorize it and recite it after every prayer.

"Allahumma A'inni Ala dhikrika wa shukrika wa husni ibaadaatika"

-- End

8. Correcting Others by "Advising" and Not "Condemning"

People always seek advice so that they can gain from others' knowledge and experience. Companies, governments, and individuals all engage in various forms of advising to move ahead and progress. Advice is also sought and given in all matters of human values pertaining to right and wrong. In general, advising others is essential for the overall betterment of groups and societies.

Providing advice by enjoining the good and forbidding the evil is an integral part of Islamic teachings. Allah says in the Quran, *"You are the best of peoples ever raised up for mankind; you enjoin Al-Ma'ruf (the good that Islam has ordained) and forbid Al-Munkar (the bad that Islam has forbidden)" Quran (Surah Aal-e-Imran:110).* He also tells us that within families, we should actively advise each other to do what's right and to stay away from the wrong. Allah says, *"O you who believe! Ward off yourselves and your families against a Fire (Hell)…" Quran (Surah At-Tehreem:6).*

As promising as the concept may seem, advising people does require a willingness and sincerity on the part of all involved. Advising takes even a different form when it is done to correct others' faults and mistakes. In personal situations, the issues can become even more delicate and complex. That is because when done incorrectly, advising people can have a reverse effect and can hurt relationships. This usually happens when one crosses the lines of "advising" people and instead "condemns" them. One can sense condemnation when the demeanor of the person seeking to correct the other appears to find fault rather than taking a sincere interest in helping the other person to rectify his faults. Sensing any feelings of condemnation, a person's ego becomes defensive to ward off any outright attempts at hurting it. We generally find people emerge from such interactions as being hurt, insulted and with soured relationships.

Here we look at issues related to correcting others and how we can make the most of such situations without demeaning each other and souring relationships in the process.

8.1 Your Role When Providing Advice

When you take on the role of pointing out other people's faults and of advising them, you have an opportunity of ensuring a positive outcome – both by ensuring that the recipient attentively listens to your advice and also by making certain that your interaction with the other person doesn't damage your relationship. You can exercise that influence by adopting the right intentions and actions and thus mitigating the risk of your advice being mistaken negatively. This will help you win the person's confidence and provide him the assurance that you could be trusted.

We should remember that while "advising" to correct someone's mistake can be helpful and beneficial to the one being advised, it involves walking a fine line, because one can cross the lines of mutual respect and get into "condemning" the other person instead. Condemning not only is the antithesis of providing sincere advice, it also constitutes a serious sin. For example, the Prophet (S.A.W.S.) even forbade the condemnation of an adulteress, though he didn't abrogate her prescribed punishment. (Based on the report in Al-Bukhaaree (4/350) and Muslim (1704) on the authority of Abu Hurairah. See Sharh-us-Sunnah (10/298) of Imaam Al-Baghawee.)

8.2 Tips To Consider When Correcting Others

Consider following some of these tips when correcting others.

Purify Your intentions: Our intentions, whether explicit or hidden, act as the catalyst in determining the final outcome of our actions. The Prophet (S.A.W.S.) said: ***"Actions are but by intentions and each person will have but that which he intended"*** (narrated by al-Bukhaari (1) and Muslim (1907)). Therefore, whenever you decide to correct and advise others, pause to ask yourself if your intent is to sincerely help the other person or to rather punish and belittle the person by exposing his defects. Surprisingly, just asking the question can reveal your hidden intentions. That will provide you an opportunity to stop yourself if you are fueled by the wrong intentions that are hidden in your psyche, which in turn can lead you on the path of "condemning" others.

Reflect the sincerity of your intentions in your demeanor: Once you are clear about your intentions, your demeanor should also reflect a sincere wish on your part to provide suggestions for improvement to the other person. It would be difficult for you to convince the other person that your intentions are pure and clean if your action and words are demeaning and punishing. Any hint of such an attitude will cause the other person to activate his defenses rather than being open and receptive to your advice. This in turn will not only lead to resentment and the weakening of your relationship but will hurt your credibility, thus locking away all future opportunities as well.

Never publicize people's faults: Unless there are valid reasons, when correcting others it is best to keep the interaction private rather than making it public. If you do it, that will make the recipient of the advice feel more humiliated and exposed. Again, if your intention is to sincerely help the other person rather than exposing his defects, the affair should be kept private. Allah (SWT) has warned us in the Quran: *"Verily, those who love that the evil and indecent actions of those who believe should be propagated (and spread), they will have a painful torment in this world and in the Hereafter. And Allah knows and you know not. And had it not been for the grace of Allah and His mercy on you, (Allah would have hastened the punishment on you) and that Allah is full of kindness, Most Merciful" Quran (Surah An-Noor:19, 20).* According to Al-Hasan, and as reported in At-Tirmidhee and other collections in marfoo' form [i.e. that the Prophet said]: *"Whosoever condemns his brother for a sin (he committed) that he repented from, will not die until he has committed it (i.e. the same sin) himself."* Al-Fudail, one of the salaf, said: *"The believer conceals (the sin of his brother) and advises (him), while the evildoer disgraces and condemns (him)."*

In this context, we should, therefore, also refrain from gossips and other idle talk that can lead us to discuss people's faults. Let us remind ourselves of the stern warnings both from Allah and His prophet about those who engage in spreading others' defects.

Don't go after looking at people's faults: While advising people of their faults with the sincere intention of correcting them is acceptable, as Muslims we are also advised not to go on a witch hunt looking after other people's faults. The prophet (S.A.W.S.) said, *"O you group of people that believe with your tongues while not with your hearts! Do not abuse the Muslims nor seek after their faults. For indeed, he who seeks after their (other people's) faults, Allah will seek after his faults. And whomsoever has Allah seek after his faults, He will expose them, even if he may have committed them in the privacy of his own home"* (reported by Abu Ya'laa in his Musnad (1675) and with a strong chain of narration in Ahmad (4/421 & 424) and Abu Dawood (4880) and other sources).

Refer people to the truth of Islam: As Muslims, when correcting someone, we should always refer them to the teachings of Islam and the prophet. This tells the other person that you are not forcing your opinions on them but rather simply reminding them about the divine commandments related to those matters. This will make the person more receptive to the advice rather than becoming defensive.

Understand the difference between 'naseehah' and 'fadeehah': *Ibn hajar in his book points out that we should be careful to note the difference between giving advice (naseehah), and disgracing the other* *(fadeehah) and taking joy in it.* The Prophet (S.A.W.S.) cautioned us when he said: **"Do not express joy at your brother's misfortune or else Allah will pardon him for it and test you with it"** (reported by multiple sources including by At-Tabaraanee in Al-Kabeer (22/53)).

This hadith therefore warns us not to rejoice at other people's misfortunes because we could be punished by it as well. Consider that when Ibn Sireen failed to return a debt he owed and was detained because of it, he said: *"Indeed, I am aware of the sin (I committed) by which this befell me. I condemned a man forty years ago saying to him: 'O bankrupt one.'"*

8.3 Advising In Personal Situations

As stated earlier, giving advice and correcting others takes on a special meaning when it is done in closer relationships, such as with close friends and family members. Sharing our day-to-day lives with others is bound to expose our faults to others more than in other situations. Furthermore, in such closer relationships where our lives are interconnected with others, one becomes more inclined to correct and advise others. The following are some of the tips that can make the process easier and less stressful:

- When correcting others, choose words that aim to "advise" rather than condemn, demean, or punish the other.
- Avoid correcting the other person when your emotions are running high. As mentioned earlier, if your intent is to see longer

term behavior change in the other person without hurting your relationship, save the advice for future when you are more in control of your emotions. Angrily advising someone is bound to push the other to erect barriers rather than staying open to listen to the advice.

- If you think that you have the right to advise others to correct their mistakes, then you also have the obligation to appreciate the good in the other person. Relationships certainly improve when you take an interest in the other person along with acknowledging and mentioning the other person's positive traits. Appreciation is the best way to reach out to the other, touch their hearts and improve your relationship. This will also lead them to put their defenses down when you need them to listen to your advice and suggestions.

- You should also be open to advice as well. When you show that you are no exception to the rules, you reveal your rational side, thus appealing to the listener and strengthening your relationship.

- Agree on a mutual protocol about advising and correcting each other. As many times, people in close relationships object to how the other advises them, setting expectations with the other person about the "when", "what", and "how" of correcting each other can prevent getting into relationship potholes.

- Even when you know that the other person is at fault, it is important to maintain humility. Consider this story which is an important reminder: The Prophet (S.A.W.S.) said: **"There were two men from Banoo Israa'eel who strove equally. One of them committed sins and the other strove hard in worship.**

And the one who strove in worship continued to see the other sinner and kept saying to him: 'Desist'. So one day, he found him committing a sin and said to him: 'Desist'. He replied: "Leave me to my Lord; have you been sent as a watcher over me?" He said: "By Allah, Allah will not forgive you, nor will Allah admit you to Paradise." Then their souls were taken and they came together before the Lord of the Worlds. So He (Allah) said to the one who strove in worship: "Did you have knowledge of Me, or did you have any power over what was in my Hands?" And He said to the sinner: "Go and enter Paradise through My Mercy." And He said to the other: "Take him to the Fire." Aboo Hurairah said: "By Him is Whose Hand is my soul! He spoke a word which destroyed this world and the Hereafter for him." (Saheeh – reported by Aboo Hurairah and collected in Aboo Daawood (Eng. trans. vol.3 p.1365 no.4883); authenticated by al-Albaanee in Saheehul-Jaami (4455)).

Finally, let us remember that in the Quran, Allah the Beneficent regards Muslims as *helpers, supporters, friends,* and *protectors* of each other: *"The believers, men and women, are Auliya' (helpers, supporters, friends, protectors) of one another"* **Quran (Surah At-Taubah:71).** Our duty, therefore, is to be genuinely concerned about each other so that we can contribute to making life pleasant in this life and to help ourselves and others to prepare for the life in the Hereafter. And to reach that end, we need to be vigilant in ensuring that Islamic teachings are implemented and followed correctly. This necessitates giving and taking correct advice and constructive criticism wherever required.

9. Ridding Oneself of Jealousy, Hatred, and Resentment

Most of us live our lives with feelings of hatred for certain people, and also with feelings of jealousy over what Allah has granted others in provisions in this life. Such feelings not only rob us of our peace within, but also hurt us both in this life and the hereafter.

It is reported in the Musnad of Ahmad from Anas, (radi-Allahu-anhu), that he said,

We were sitting in the presence of the Messenger of Allah (s.a.w.) one day and he said, `A person is about to arrive from this mountain path who is from the people of Paradise.' So a person from the Ansar arrived, his beard dripping with the water of wudu and holding his sandals in his left hand, and he gave us the salam. The next day the Prophet (s.a.w.) said similar words and the same person appeared in the same condition. On the third day the Prophet (s.a.w.) again said similar words and again this person appeared in the same condition, so when the Prophet (s.a.w.) left, `Abdullah bin `Amr al-Aas followed this person and said, indeed I have abused my father and I swore that I would not go to him for three days so if you would let me stay with you until those three days expire, I would do so.' He replied, `Yes.'

Anas continued saying,

So `Abdullah told us that he spent three nights with this person yet he did not see him stand for the night prayer at all. All he did was when he turned sides on his bed he would mention Allah and make takbir and would do this until he stood for the Fajr prayer. `Abdullah said, `Except that I never heard him speak except good.' So when the three days were over I was eager to make little of his actions. I said, `O servant of Allah there was no hatred or disassociation between my father and me but I heard the Messenger of Allah (saying on three occasions, `A person is about to arrive who is from the people of Paradise,' and you arrived on those three occasions, so I wished to stay with you so that I may look at your actions and emulate them. But I have not seen you perform a great deal of actions, so what is it that has reached you to make the Messenger of Allah (s.a.w.) say what he said?' He replied, `It is nothing more than what you have seen, except that I do not find in myself any disloyalty (animosity) toward any of the Muslims, and neither do I find any jealousy for the wealth that Allah has bestowed upon them.' [Musnad of Ahmad from Anas]

We can see from the above hadith that keeping a clean heart rather than one filled with hatred, jealousy, and animosity can be a source of peace in this life and salvation on the day of judgment.

In our daily dealings with people, some of us not only have such feelings about others but we also forsake them because of those feelings. We should remind ourselves that it is not permissible to forsake a Muslim, because the Prophet (peace and blessings of Allah be upon him) said: *"it is not permissible for a man to forsake his Muslim brother for more than three days, each of them turning away from the other when they meet. the better of them is the one who gives the greeting of salaam first."* (Narrated by al-Bukhaari, 5727; Muslim, 2560). This applies especially if the believer is a relative because forsaking relatives is an even greater sin.

We learn from scholars that the only exception of this is in cases where the other's company and mixing can hurt one spiritually and in other areas of one's life. Ibn 'Abd al-Barr also said: *"The scholars are unanimously agreed that it is not permissible for a Muslim to forsake his brother for more than three days, unless there is the fear that speaking to him and keeping in touch with him will affect one's religious commitment or have some harmful effect on one's spiritual and worldly interests. If that is the case, it is permissible to avoid him, because peaceful avoidance is better than harmful mixing."* (Tarh al-Tathreeb, 8/99)

The general principle is that *"the Muslim must be forbearing and sincere towards his brothers, he must be tolerant towards them and overlook their mistakes. He should not hasten to adopt a solution that may cause division and haraam kinds of forsaking."* (islamqa.info)

9.1 Feeling Jealous Of Other's Provisions And Rizq

To avoid feelings of jealousy of the provisions that others may have, we should remind ourselves that Allah has apportioned our provisions in this life and that feeling jealous of others is akin to disagreeing with Allah on His decisions. Consider the following verses from the Quran:

"Is it they who would portion out the Mercy of your Lord? It is We Who portion out between them their livelihood in this world, and We raised some of them above others in ranks, so that some may employ others in their work. But the Mercy of your Lord is better than the (wealth of this world) which they amass." Quran (Surah Az-Zukhruf:32)

In a hadith narrated by Al-Tirmidhi from al-Zubayr ibn al-'Awaam that the Prophet (S.A.W.S.) said:

"There has come to you the disease of the nations before you, jealousy and hatred. This is the 'shaver' (destroyer); I do not say that it shaves hair, but that it shaves (destroys) faith. By the One in Whose Hand is my soul, you will not enter Paradise until you believe, and you will not believe until you love one another. Shall I not tell you of that which will strengthen love between you? Spread (the greeting of) salaam amongst yourselves." (A hasan hadeeth. Jaami' al-Tirmidhi, 2434).

9.2 Cleaning Our Hearts Of Jealousy And Hatred

As part of our personal purification efforts, we should constantly work to rid our hearts of such feelings. No one is free from such feelings, but we should venture to avoid Satan's whispers which instill these kinds of negative feelings in our hearts. Shaykh al-Islam Ibn Taymiyah said: *"Nobody is free from hasad (jealousy), but the noble person hides it whilst the base person shows it."* (Amraad al-Quloob). A person will not be brought to account for whatever crosses his mind, but he will be brought to account for what he says and does. The Prophet (peace and blessings of Allah be upon him) said: **"Allah will forgive my ummah (nation) for their mistakes, what they forget and what they are forced to do."** (Narrated by al-Bukhaari, 2033).

Shaykh al-Islam Ibn Taymiyah also said in his book Amraad al-Quloob (diseases of the heart): *"Whoever finds in himself any hasad towards another has to try to neutralize it by means of taqwa (piety, consciousness of Allah) and sabr (patience). So he should hate that (the feeling of hasad) in himself… But the one who does wrong to his brother by word or deed will be punished for that. The one who fears Allah and is patient, however, is not included among the wrongdoers, and Allah will benefit him by his taqwa."*

-- End

10. Not losing hope in the Du'as that we make

One of the common complaints of many of us Muslims is that when we make Du'a, we don't see its immediate effects. As a result, we get disheartened and lose hope in the effectiveness and powers of our Du'a. This article highlights wisdom from a passage written by Ibn Al-Jawzi (may Allah have mercy on him) where he discusses this topic.

For those of us who don't know, Abu'l-Faraj ibn al-Jawzi (508 AH – 597 AH) is known to be one of the most prolific authors in Islamic history. According to research conducted on the extent of his research works, the number of Ibn al-Jawzi's books is greater than 376 texts. Some even say that he is the author of more than 700 works.

About the matter of Du'as not being answered, Ibn al-Jawzi, in one of his books, makes the following comment:

"I think part of the test is when a believer supplicates and receives no response, and he repeats the Du'a for a long time and sees no sign of a response. He should realize that this is a test and needs patience.

What a person experiences of waswaas (whispers from shaytan) when the response is delayed is a sickness which needs medicine. I have experienced this myself. A calamity befell me and I supplicated and did not see any response, and Iblees started to lay his traps. Sometimes he said: The generosity (of Allah) is abundant and He is not miserly, so why is there a delay?

I said to him: Be gone, O cursed one, for I have no need of anyone to argue my case and I do not want you as a supporter!

Then I told myself: Beware of going along with his whispers, for if there was no other reason for the delay except that Allah is testing you to see whether you will fight the enemy, that is sufficient wisdom.

My soul (nafs) said: How could you explain the delay in the response of Allah to your prayers for relief from this calamity?

I said: It is proven with evidence that Allah, may He be glorified and exalted, is the Sovereign, and the Sovereign may withhold or give, so there is no point in objecting to Him.

The wisdom behind that is proven in definitive evidence. I may think that something is good, but wisdom does not dictate it, but the reason for that may be hidden, just as a doctor may do things that appear outwardly to be harmful, intending some good purpose thereby. Perhaps this is something of that nature.

There may be an interest to be served by delay, and haste may be harmful. The Prophet (peace and blessings of Allah be upon him) said: **"A person will be fine so long as he does not become impatient and says, 'I prayed but I did not receive any answer.'"**

The response may be withheld because of some fault in you. Perhaps there was something dubious in what you ate or your heart was heedless at the time when you said the Du'a, or your punishment is being increased by means of your need being withheld, because of some sin from which you have not repented sincerely. So look for some of these reasons, so that you might achieve your aim.

You should examine the intention behind this request, because attaining it may lead to more sin, or prevent you from doing some good, so withholding it is better.

Perhaps losing what you have missed out on will cause you to turn to Allah and getting it will distract you from Him. This is obvious, based on the fact that were it not for this calamity you would not have turned to Him, because the real calamity is what distracts you from Him, but what makes you stand before Him is good for you and is in your best interests.

If you ponder these things you will focus on what is more beneficial for you, such as correcting a mistake or seeking forgiveness or standing before Allah and beseeching Him, and forget about what you have missed out on." (Sayd al-Khaatir (59-60) This publication is in three volumes containing aphorisms and wise counsels.)

About the issue of Du'as being accepted, the following two sayings by Prophet Muhammad (S.A.W.S.) are also very noteworthy:

It was narrated that Faddalah ibn 'Ubayd said: The Prophet (peace and blessings of Allah be upon him) heard a man making Du'a after his prayer, but he did not send blessings upon the Prophet (peace and blessings of Allah be upon him). The Prophet (peace and blessings of Allah be upon him) said: "This man is in a hurry." Then he called him and said to him or to someone else: "When any

one of you has finished praying (and makes dua), let him start by praising Allah, then let him send blessings upon the Prophet (peace and blessings of Allah be upon him), then after that let him ask for whatever he wants." (Saheeh Sunan al-Tirmidhi, 2765. Al-Albani classed it as a saheeh hadeeth.)

The Prophet (peace and blessings of Allah be upon him) also said:

"The slave will receive a response so long as his Du'a does not involve sin or severing of family ties, and so long as he is not hasty." It was said, "What does being hasty mean?" He said: "When he says, 'I made Du'a and I made Du'a, and I have not seen any response,' and he gets frustrated and stops making du'a." Narrated by al-Bukahari, 6340; Muslim, 2735.

In conclusion, for those of us who have abandoned the practice of Du'a, we may be missing something quite important. Wishing for something is not the same thing as asking Allah by making a Du'a. We may keep wishing our wishes but we have a better chance of seeing them materialized when we actually make the effort to enter the state of Du'a and asking Allah what we want.

-- End

11. Managing Relationships

Relationships are the lifeblood of our journey through this world. Good relationships can not only help us to navigate through the challenges of this life with greater ease, but they can also be fulfilling and invigorating. Bad relationships, on the other hand, can stop one's life dead in its tracks. Ask a divorced person who has left a married life – or a person who has needed to change his work due to bad relationships – or ask family members who have been left devastated and shattered because of family squabbles. They will all attest to the powerful, yet negative impact of bad relationships, and their ability to alter the course of one's life, often leaving them debilitated in the process.

It's a no-brainer that good relationships can provide the energy that allows our lives to bloom. Building and maintaining good relationships is an art as well as a science, the underlying principles of which come together in a mesmerizing way, making it one of the most important subjects for the human species. Whether realized earlier in life, or discovered later through the heat of experience, one eventually comes to grips with the fact that the principles of relationships must be learned – and when mastered effectively, these principles can enable one to use good judgment; to become more empathetic; become more sensitive to human emotions to better understand personalities, and so much more. All of a sudden, with these principles in place, life changes, feels less complicated, more fulfilling, and more controlled.

But one wonders why we humans have made this important and promising pursuit, that of building and maintaining superb relationships, not only very complex, convoluted and confusing, but almost unmanageable: many of us fail miserably even at the very basics. It is no wonder, then, that books on relationships sell more than any other specific topic. Even more baffling is the fact that many of us Muslims fail to follow the ready-made recipes that Islam provides us, along with the living example of the Prophet Muhammad (S.A.W.S.), who among many other things was a master of human relationships. So, a review of the basics is in order.

11.1 Some Relationships Can Involve Pain

No one would argue against the suggestion that being in relationships has the potential to cause enormous mental pain and agony. Whether it's one spouse verbally assaulting the other spouse, a child defying parents and family values, friends violating a trust, or a supervisor putting an employee down, these relationship potholes can wreck our souls, which can cause us to get a heavy heart and a burdened mind, can make us cry and feel frustrated and indifferent. Ultimately, at times, all of these negative emotions which result from poorly managed relationships can leave us questioning the value of such relationships in the first place. What's worse is that, when we continue to live in such relationships, we rob our lives of the energy and the enthusiasm that could otherwise have shaped our lives in a different, more positive way, than that which it ultimately becomes.

The "blame game" rules such relationships. One's ego is the master. People's self-worth is trampled on. Others are at fault. Justice is not present. Life does not seem "fair". One feels victimized. Insensitivity to feelings rules, and the emotional rollercoaster seems endless.

Such relationships are in need of serious repair.

11.2 Relationships Can Be Pleasing And Fulfilling

On the flip side, healthy relationships can be extremely rewarding. Ask a parent about how proud they feel to have raised good and respectful children. Ask a husband or wife about the respect they get from each other, and the way that that makes them feel. Ask fast friends about the trust they have for each other. Ask strong business partners about the respect they have for each other and so on. Love, trust, and respect uplift our souls, make our lives more fulfilling and meaningful, and make us thankful for our relationships. All of these positive modes of relating create reciprocated, mutual good feelings.

Not only do such relationships need to be cherished, but, more importantly, they need to be actively maintained.

11.3 Relationships Must Be Actively Managed

So, how do we manage the pain and pleasure which is associated with such relationships? It's actually quite simple – in theory at least. You manage a relationship by actively working on it, and by constantly renewing it. If you are even a moderately practicing Muslim, you know how that works. You know that the relationship with your Creator is the most important one. Even in those cases, the relationship must be renewed.

Consider the saying of the Prophet (S.A.W.S.) who said, *"Faith wears out in your heart as clothes wear out, so ask Allah to renew the faith in your hearts." (narrated by al-Haakim in his Mustadrak and al-Tabaraani in his Mu'jam with a saheeh isnaad).*

So, again – you manage relationships by actively working on them. And that means that if you are having challenges with your relationships, you should step out of your "default mode" of dealing with relationships. The "default" mode is how most of us learn and develop subconsciously while growing up. In that mode, we are mentally wired to deal with people and relationships in general. The better our relationships were managed at home while growing up, the better our default mode will be and the better we will be able to build and maintain good relationships with others, our spouses, and other acquaintances, in our adult lives. Growing up while observing families in lousy relationships can makes one's default mode develop in the same manner – creating a manner of relating that other people can't live with – unless of course one takes concrete steps to change those learned behaviors. For example, did you know that research has established that most criminals come from broken homes, where they were abused as children while growing up? Although this scary fact applies to only a small fraction of people, it serves to illustrate the point that when unchecked, bad relationships can lead to devastating consequences.

Shifting out of your default mode of dealing with relationships is about making a purposeful change in your attitude toward other people – a change that others can notice – it's about expressing your appreciation, and doing things for others. For some of us making this change can be easy, and for some, it's not.

Ideally, one should start learning the basics of building and maintaining good relationships from early childhood. It is no wonder that a number of schools now have adopted a curriculum that teaches building good relationship skills right from pre-school years. In parallel, parents should strive to maintain a healthy social environment at home. Although no formal research has yet been done on this topic, many observations attest to the unfortunate fact that in most Muslim countries, the awareness for such education is far less than that which exists in western societies. That is very unfortunate, considering the fact that the life of the Prophet (S.A.W.S.) is exemplary in demonstrating how well he treated people, families, children, and how much he encouraged parents to treat children with kindness.

Once children are raised in homes where they are taught to respect and manage their relationships, it in turn helps them to grow up to be strong individuals, as they become adept at building and maintaining very strong relationships with people in all walks of life. With practice, doing so becomes second nature, and helps the person in relationships with family, friends and work. The "default mode" of such people, given the correct example, thus turns out to be quite healthy.

Have you ever wondered about what your default mode is in dealing with people? Do your loved ones cherish your behavior or do they run from your verbal assaults? Reflect on this hadith: **'Abdullah bin 'Amr bin Al-'As, may Allah be pleased with them, said: A person asked Allah's Messenger (may peace and blessings be upon him) who among Muslims was better. Upon this (the Holy Prophet) remarked: One from whose hand and tongue Muslims are safe.**

So, assess your default mode of dealing with people, family members, and friends – if you don't like it and if you believe that your loved ones also don't like it too, maybe it's time to consider making some changes immediately.

Once you start making the change, you will notice that it is not rocket science. In fact, most of you exercise those skills in business settings regularly. For example, what will you do to maintain a good business relationship that is very vital for your business and income? More commonly it involves some of the following:

- Being empathetic to your clients' needs – listening with an open mind and heart
- Being very serious and sincere to avoid and clarify any misunderstandings
- Going out of your way to be appreciative of the relationship that you have with them
- Going out of your way to be apologetic

- Always keeping a pleasing and charming attitude
- And so on.

Many of us in our business and professional dealings do the above, and more, as required, constantly. The sense of purpose in the need to keep our business going and flourishing, makes us not only do the above but makes many of us come up with the most creative and innovative ways to keep our business partners happy. It's a no-brainer. It's common sense.

But not very surprisingly, the same "brain" and "sense" starts to malfunction when it comes to personal relationships within our families. That's where something gets lost in the process. So, it's not that we do not know how to manage relationships – we just don't apply them in all settings and situations.

11.4 Prioritize Your Relationships

Do you know anyone who spends more time strengthening relationships with their friends and business partners than their own families? Does that make sense? Let us face it – certain relationships are more important than others, and therefore deserve more time and effort than others. For example, it would just not make sense for you to hold your friends in high respect while you mistreat your parents. You can't abandon your own children whilst helping other children. Charity always begins at home.

Even in Islam which teaches respect, love, patience and understanding as the cornerstone of all relationships, certain relationships are given more priority over others. There are numerous accounts in the Quran and Hadith about the importance given to certain relations. For example, in a well-known hadith, **Abu Hurayrah (may Allah be pleased with him) said: "A man came to the Messenger of Allah (peace and blessings of Allah be upon him) and said, 'O Messenger of Allah, who among the people is most deserving of my good companionship?' He said, 'Your mother.' The man asked, 'Then who?' He said, 'Your mother.' He asked, then who?' He said, 'Your mother.' He asked, 'Then who?' He said, 'Your father.'"**

It is also reported, on the authority of Ayesha (R.A.) and Ibn Umar (R.A.) that the messenger of Allah, **Prophet Muhammad (PBUH) said "The Angel Jibra'il (A.S.) counseled me so frequently regarding the rights of the neighbor that I feared, he too would be declared an heir."**

Just because you are "around" your family members more, doesn't mean that you should spend the least amount of time nurturing those relationships.

Allah says (interpretation of the meaning): "Would you then, if you were given the authority, do mischief in the land, and sever your ties of kinship? Such are they whom Allah has cursed, so that He has made them deaf and blinded their sight" Quran (Surah Muhammad:22,23)

And the Prophet (peace and blessings of Allah be upon him) said: "No one who severs the ties of kinship will enter Paradise." Narrated by Muslim in his Saheeh.

11.5 Relationships Can Be Repaired

If you take a look around you, you won't have to look far to see a broken home, or a community at odds with itself. Everyone probably knows someone (if not within our own circles) who walks around angry at someone, hurt by someone, frustrated with someone, irritated by others, and sick of life in general.

These kinds of relationships, ones that involve people holding grudges against others, accompanied by emotional rollercoasters, verbal assaults and emotional outbursts, obviously involve a lot of pain and thus need an active reparation process.

More often than not, spousal relationship topics top all other forms of relationships that need repair. So, it needs specific mention. How would you classify your relationship with your spouse? Is it bad or routine at best? Once relationships become routine, spouses in a troubled relationship are less forgiving, they amplify mistakes, and throw verbal assaults more often than they are cheerful to each other. What one spouse does for the other as part of a routine activity of running household errands, working to make a living, raising children, etc. is taken for granted. For example, in homes where the wife is the home maker, "appreciation" does not cross the wife's mind for her husband working hard to make a living, and the husband does not see anything extraordinary in the mother keeping the house on track and raising children.

As the focus in such "boring-to-get-worse-soon" relationships shifts from the good to the bad and even more to the ugly, there is a need to break that thinking pattern and to start focusing on the "good". With time, the tendency is to start ignoring the qualities and instead to focus on the negatives. **The Prophet Muhammad (peace and blessings of Allah be upon him) said: "No believing man should hate a believing woman: if he dislikes one of her characteristics, he will like another." (Reported by Muslim, 36). The Prophet (S.A.W.S.) also said as narrated by Abu Hurairah: "He who does not thank people, does not thank Allah". (Ahmad, Tirmidhi)**

So, sprinkle a few words of understanding and appreciation in the routine or not so routine relationships and you will see your relationships improve, feel your hearts clamed and your souls less jittery. You just can't repair a relationship without these basics – else, you either get a boring relationship or could even be headed for more trouble.

-- End

11.6 Relationships Are Defined By A Person's Character

A person's strength is, in many ways, a reflection of the strength of his or her relationships. A person who is weak succumbs to unbridled emotions, uncontrolled anger and erratic thought processes. These are, in turn, a perfect recipe for poisoning relationships. Contrary to some misunderstood cultural beliefs, uncontrolled anger and emotional outbursts show a person's weakness rather than his "manly" attributes. Such a character stems from a person's upbringing, which lacked focus on Islamic values. The truth as Islam teaches us is that a strong person manages his emotions and directs them appropriately to build and manage relationships rather than using them to damage relationships.

To get a glimpse of how anger should be handled, we need to study the life of the Prophet (S.A.W.S.). When we study the prophet's behavior and the behavior of his companions, we will likely understand that verbal assaults are NOT the way to manage anger. But obviously, when we are weak, we succumb to the whims and desires of the untrained mind, and in the process unleash such aggressive, damaging behavior. Abu Hurairah narrated that Prophet Muhammad (S.A.W.S.) said: *"The strong man is not the one who is strong in wrestling, but the one who controls himself in anger"* (Bukhari, Muslim).

11.7 The Ultimate Relationship Is The One With Our Creator

Finally, let us not forget that the ultimate relationship that any one of us can have is that with our Creator. Establishing such a relationship is the cornerstone of an Islamic faith. Such a relationship also helps fill the gap left out by the anxieties, loneliness, depressions and other emotional extremes and rollercoasters that one goes through in life.

In a Hadith the Prophet (PBUH) said that Allah said: *"...my servant does not come closer to Me with anything more dear to Me than that which I made obligatory upon him. My servant keeps coming closer to Me with more volunteer deeds, until I love him. When I love him, I become His ear by which he hears, his eyes by which he sees, his hand by which he holds and his foot by which he walks. If he asks Me anything I shall give him. If he seeks My protection I shall grant him My protection... "(Al-Bukhari 6021)*

11.8 Use Good Old Common Sense

Before closing, we all need to remind ourselves that building and managing healthy relationships and avoiding the potholes of bad relationships involves the use of basic common sense. Stepping away from the heat of the moment – correcting others respectfully without destroying their self-worth – disassociating oneself from negative emotions – reflecting on the cause and effect behavior that shapes good and bad relationships, and other such basics, can bring about clarity and a change in our attitudes. It can help us break the pattern that we can get repeatedly pulled into. Remember, what Einstein said – *"The definition of stupidity is doing the same thing over and over again and expecting different results"*. If your relationships are bad, then change how you are contributing to those relationships. You will be surprised to see how things change.

If we think and reflect, we will begin to get the answers to the common day-to-day problems that many of us face in our daily lives. We will learn that in close relationships, sometimes love and respect need to supersede the desire to prove oneself right and the other wrong. Some more thinking and reflection will lead us to the fact that a daughter-in-law's and mother-in-law's relationship can rarely be strong if the man in the middle does not have a good relationship with both. We will learn that children ought to be taught the essentials of relationships early on in their life – something that an Islamic education will teach more than their secular education. Thinking and reflection will make it dawn on us that love and respect in most cases needs to be earned by one's own behavior and not demanded and forced. And the list can go on...

Finally, if you think these tips apply only to others and not to your situation – think again. The foundation of most of these insights was taught by our Prophet (S.A.W.S.) and he came with practical guidelines for humanity at large. Understanding this is where we may need to become strong and change our attitudes.

-- End

12. The Sin of Riya (Showing Off)

'Riya' refers to doing things that are pleasing to Allah with the intention of seeking admiration from others. The intention in such cases, therefore, is usually to show off one's good deeds in order to win the praise and admiration of others. It amounts to practicing virtue out of vanity, with the sole aim of achieving popularity among people.

Riya makes us focus on earning appreciation from people rather than seeking Allah's favor and acceptance. It makes us focus on people's appreciation of our virtuous acts, which means we give importance to them, and not to Allah the Most Benevolent.

Considering the temporary nature of things, our chief concern should rather be on the long-term rewards, and thus to do good to earn Allah's pleasure, because that alone can benefit us both in this world and the next.

But Satan knows how easy it is to fill our hearts with vanity, and he arouses in us the desire for a good name and reputation, making our deeds fruitless, by distancing us from Allah.

The Prophet (S.A.W.S.) described *Riya'* by giving the example of a person performing prayer for Allah, and improving his rendering of the *Salat* when he knows that others are watching him. Allah says:

So woe unto those performers of Salat (hypocrites), Those who delay their Salat (from their stated fixed times). <u>Those who do</u>

good deeds only to be seen (of men). *And prevent Al-Ma'un (small kindnesses)* **Quran (Surah Al-Maauun:4 – 7)**

12.1 Doing Good Deeds For Worldly Reasons Is Minor Shirk

In Majmoo' Fataawa wa Maqaalaat Mutanawwi'ah, Shaykh al-Allaamah Abd al-Azeez ibn Abd-Allah ibn Baaz, (may Allah have mercy on him) stated that *"Any good deed performed with the intention of showing off and pleasing people is not acceptable. For example, if one reads the Quran craving for people's admiration for the beautiful recitation and not as a duty to Allah, this behavior falls under the category of showing off, and is considered minor shirk. We should, therefore, be aware of such shirk and do every good deed for Allah alone, and not to enhance our image or status among people."* (Vol. 9, p. 3.)

We know that on the Day of Judgment we will be in desperate need of Allah's mercy. We can get His mercy on that day by focusing today on doing good deeds for His sake alone. Instead, when we do good deeds to seek others' admiration, Allah will turn us away. The Messenger of Allah, (S.A.W.S.) said,

"Verily, what I fear most for you is the lesser idolatry." **And he elaborated,** *"It is showing off. Allah the Exalted will say to them (who show off), on the Day of Resurrection when the people are being rewarded for their deeds: Go to those whom you wished to*

show off in the world and look for your reward with them." **(Musnad Ahmad Hadith 23119)**

Abu Sa'id Al-Khudri reported: The Messenger of Allah (S.A.W.S.), entered upon us while we were discussing the False Messiah. He said,

"Shall I not tell you about what I fear for you more than the presence of the False Messiah?" **We said, "Of course!" He said,** *"Hidden idolatry; that a man stands for prayer and beautifies his prayer because he sees another man looking at him."* **(Ibn Majah Hadith 4202)**

12.2 Punishment in the Hereafter

People are more likely to commit this sin if they are ignorant of the manner in which this will be punished in the Hereafter. We must realize that it cancels out the reward of all our good deeds, and brings on us the wrath of Allah. No sensible person would like to waste energy doing that which doesn't bring any reward, and certainly wouldn't like to invite Allah's anger. One of the greatest ahadith in this connection is the following (part of the long hadith stated below):

Abu Hurairah (R.A) narrated a hadith of the Messenger of Allah (S.A.W.S.) that clearly shows how the act of doing things for others can cause some to be enflamed on the Day of Judgment. One of them, for example, will be a wealthy man who will be brought, and Allah will say to him: "Was I not so generous with

you that I did not leave you without any need from anyone?" He will reply: 'Of course O Lord!' Allah will ask: "Then what did you do with what I gave to you?" He will say: 'I would nurture the ties of kinship and give charity.' Then Allah will say to him: "You have lied. Rather, you wanted it to be said that so-and-so is so generous, and that was said. (Meaning that you wanted to get appreciated and that's what happened.)" (Part of a long hadith in Sunan Tirmidhi Vol. 4, Book 10, Hadith 2382).

Again, such are the people who, according to the prophet (S.A.W.S.), will face severe punishment in the hereafter.

12.3 Punishment in This World

Just as there will be a punishment in the Hereafter for showing off, so will there be one in this world. We learn that from the prophet who told us that Allah will expose the person and his bad intentions. The Messenger (S.A.W.S.) said:

"If anyone wants to have his deeds widely publicized, Allah will publicize (his humiliation). And if anyone makes a hypocritical display (of his deeds) Allah will make a display of him." (Saheeh Muslim Book 42, Hadith 7115)

12.4 Causes and Cures

Before discussing some of the cures for this disease, let us focus on some of the things which may contribute to Riya in the first place.

Weakness of faith (Eeman) – When a person doesn't have strong faith in Allah, he'll prefer the admiration of people over the pleasure of Allah.

Fear of criticism – One might make a display of his good deeds to avoid being criticized. For example, a person might pray in the mosque out of fear of being criticized by people for not doing it.

Envy of people's possessions – Giving undue importance to worldly possessions and coveting what others have by way of status, position, or wealth urges one to show off his own acquisitions.

To ward off the temptation of showing off, one should focus on the following:

Remember That Allah Is Always Watching Him

Awareness of standing before Allah (SWT) is the status of "ihsaan" (perfection in worship). Abu Hurairah reported that in answer to a man's question about 'Ihsaan' the Prophet (S.A.W.S.) explained, *"Ihsan is to worship Allah as if you see Him, and if you do not achieve this state of devotion, then (take it for granted that) Allah sees you."* (Saheeh Bukhari Vol. 6, Book 60, Hadith 300).

Consciousness of Allah arouses in us respect and fear of Allah. What other people think then becomes insignificant. Undue concern about this world is fruitless. The more importance we give it, the more it entangles us in a web of never ending desires and ever expanding ambitions that traps one in the fleeting pleasures of this transitory world. With a heart inclined towards preparation for the eternal life, one has to seek the pleasure of Allah before leaving the world and entering the grave.

Conceal Worship And Not Make A Display Of It

Satan is always on the lookout for the one who shows any inclination and weakness towards impressing others, and he arouses in him the desire for Riya. One can counter this by making a conscious effort to not publicize his or her noble deeds, unless it is obligatory, such as praying in congregation for men, etc. Care should also be taken to not make any difference in one's prayers, simply because of the presence or absence of others

The Prophet (S.A.W.S.) said, *"He who lets the people hear of his good deeds intentionally, to win their praise, Allah will let people know his real intention (on the Day of Resurrection), and he who does good things in public to show off and win the praise of the people, Allah will disclose his real intention (and humiliate him)."* (Saheeh Bukhari Vol. 8, Book 76, Hadith 506)

Reflect Upon One's Own Shortcomings

Besides not giving importance to the opinion of people, one should keep a constant check on one's own shortcomings. Awareness of our weaknesses is a sure way of keeping our feet firmly planted on the earth, and of not allowing us to get carried away by any praise that comes our way. By thanking Allah All Mighty for our achievements, we become conscious that it is He Alone Who makes us capable of all that we might achieve, and this effectively curbs the desire to take credit for our good deeds.

Seek Allah's Help In Overcoming Riya

Allah, the Most Merciful, knows every human's weakness and has given us the cure as well. The best means is supplication to Him. Allah says that we should say (which means):

"**You (Alone) we worship, and You (Alone) we ask for help (for each and everything)**" Quran (Surah Al-Fatihah:5)

This Aayah from Surah Al-Fatihah should strengthen our faith and make us steadfast. When we say that we worship Allah Alone, we should follow up this assertion with our actions. Worship signifies obedience and trust. It naturally follows that our deeds should have Allah's acceptance as their only goal. Desire for worldly praise should be discarded.

"Neeyah", intention – the deciding factor

We should not let fear of Riya take us to the other extreme, and therefore to prevent us from doing good. Just as Satan arouses in us vanity and the yearning for self-glorification, he also uses his wiles to make us avoid doing good out of fear of showing off. This suspicion can weaken our resolve, and eventually stop us from doing that which pleases Allah. An honest assessment of the purity of our *'neeyah'* (intention) can help us in such a situation. We should ensure that the intention to seek Allah's favor is the only factor that drives us in the practice of good. As long as we are sincere in our intentions, we need not worry about anything that Satan might come up with. A heart fortified with strong faith and sincerity of intention is not troubled by Satan's whispers, when practicing virtues secretly or openly.

Ibraheem Al-Nakha'l said: *"If Satan comes to you when you are praying and says, "You are showing off," then you should make it even longer." Shaykh Ibn 'Uthaymeen (may Allah have mercy on him) suggested that seeking Allah's refuge from the accursed Satan, one should go ahead with the good deed and not pay attention to his discouraging waswasaas (whispers from Satan).* (Majmoo' Fataawa Al-Shaykh Ibn 'Uthaymeen, Question No. 277)

In conclusion, let us remind ourselves that he purpose of a Muslim's life is to become a "Muhsin" – a doer of good deeds who performs his actions totally for Allah, in accordance with the Sunnah of Allah's Messenger (S.A.W.S.), without any desire for worldly gain, praise or fame. Allah the Most Exalted praises such believers in several Ayahs of the Quran. He (SWT) says, (which means):

"… but whoever submits his face (himself) to Allah (i.e. follows Allah's Religion of Islamic Monotheism) and he is a Muhsin then his reward is with his Lord (Allah), on such shall be no fear, nor shall they grieve". Quran (Surah Al-Baqara:112)

"…And who has (in mind) no favor from anyone to be paid back. Except to seek the Face of his Lord, the Most High." Quran (Surah Al-Layl:19, 20)

Narrated 'Âishah that the Prophet (S.A.W.S.) said, **"Do good deeds properly, sincerely and moderately, and receive good news because one's good deeds will not make him enter Paradise."** They asked, "Even you, O Allah's Messenger?" He said, **"Even I, unless and until Allah protects or covers me with His pardon and His Mercy."** (Saheeh Al-Bukhâri, Vol.8, Hadîth No.474).

So, we see that entry into Paradise depends totally on the pardon, mercy and acceptance of Allah the Most Forgiving; rejoicing in worldly praise and feeling secure in our virtuous acts is self-deception; it is for Allah to accept them.

Finally, we can memorize a Du'a to help us stay away from shirk. The Prophet (S.A.W.S.) said**: "O people, beware of this shirk (form of polytheism), for it is more subtle than the footsteps of an ant."** When a person asked, "How can we beware of it when it is more *subtle than the footsteps of an ant, O Messenger of Allah?" He said, "Say:*

Allahumma innee a'oodhu bika min an ushrika bika shai'aun wa ana a'lamu wa astaghfiruka limaa laa a'alamu"

O Allah, we seek refuge with You from knowingly associating anything with You, and we seek Your forgiveness for that which we do unknowingly." (Musnad Ahmad Hadith 19171)

-- End

13. The Islamic Etiquette Of Dealing With People

Islamic teachings place great emphasis on how we deal with people in our daily lives. The prophet (S.A.W.S.) summed up his message by stating: *"I have been sent to perfect the best of manners"*. As Muslims, we, therefore, have to be aware of how each one of us deals with the people in our circles. Our good dealings will not only ensure that we are not violating other people's rights, but can also make us accepted, loved and appreciated by others. Luqman once said to his son, *"O my son: Let your speech be good and your face be smiling; you will be more loved by the people than those who give them provisions."* (Mentioned in the stories of ibn Kathir.)

Experience shows that life becomes pleasant when we can manage our work and relationships well. Quranic wisdom and the example of Prophet Muhammad's (S.A.W.S.) dealings with people should help us steer our relationships and keep them on the right track. This article highlights certain essential principles of Islam that guide us in this matter.

13.1 Not Showing Pride And Arrogance

It is quite easy to get carried away by whatever we may possess in the way of wealth and the good things of life. It is so easy and common to credit ourselves with our achievements, and to feel proud of them, and then, as a matter of course, to look down upon others who haven't been able to put in the same effort or reach the status we might have achieved. It is our own ego, and the ever opportunistic Satan who knows our vulnerability, which makes us take on such an attitude. And so The One Who cares the most for our well-being, Allah the Most Merciful, has warned us against falling into the trap of pride and arrogance. He says in the Quran (interpretation of the Arabic meaning):

And turn not your face away from men with pride, nor walk in insolence through the earth. Verily, Allah likes not any arrogant boaster. Quran (Surah Luqman:18)

The way to avoid pride and arrogance is to remember Allah as much as we can, until it becomes a habit to thank Him instantly for any good that comes our way. Thankfulness to Allah creates humility in us, and makes us aware that we are not entirely responsible for all the good things of life, or for the status which we enjoy. We wouldn't have gotten them if He hadn't willed them for us, nor can we retain them if He decides to take them away from us.

13.2 Not Mocking Others

We often see people taking pleasure in mocking others. Is it that the ego craves for the satisfaction of proving oneself better than others by looking out for others' weaknesses and laughing at them? But Allah admonishes us in the following verse:

O you who believe! Let not a group scoff at another group, it may be that the latter are better than the former. Nor let (some) women scoff at other women, it may be that the latter are better than the former. Quran (Surah Hujrat:11)

Allah tells us that our knowledge is restricted by our limited perception. Since we are not aware of any one's real worth, wouldn't it be foolish to laugh at those who might actually be better than us? We can curb this tendency to humiliate others by opening our eyes to the fact that when we think that others deserve to be ridiculed, we are actually fooling ourselves, and no one else (though we might find a few thoughtless and insensitive people to give us company in our foolish pastime).

13.3 Not Addressing People With Undesirable Titles

A general misconception about someone's sense of humor is their so called 'ability' to make others laugh. Giving nicknames to others on account of some negative characteristic that is noticed in them or even some disability that they might be suffering from is a crude form of entertainment. Making fun of those who stammer, or are very short or lean, is obviously some form of indecency practiced by callous people, and enjoyed by others who lack sensitivity to human feelings. Allah warns us against such behavior and practices. He says:

"... Nor defame yourselves, nor insult one another by nicknames. Evil is the name of wickedness after faith. And whosoever does not repent, then such are indeed wrongdoers." Quran (Surah Hujrat:11)

13.4 Refraining From 'Tajassus' (Spying)

Imam Al-Nawawi (rh) said that scholars have differentiated between 'tahassus', which means 'snooping' and listening to other people's conversations, and 'tajassus', which means 'spying', seeking out other people's faults and looking for secrets. Both activities are considered evil and have been forbidden. Allah Says:

"O you who believe! Avoid much suspicion; indeed some suspicion is sin. And spy not, neither backbite one another. Would one of you like to eat the flesh of his dead brother? You would hate it. And have Taqwa of Allah. Verily, Allah is the One Who forgives and accepts repentance, Most Merciful." Quran (Surah Al-Hujrat:12)

Is it for want of a better activity to keep ourselves busy, that we enjoy peeping into others' lives?

Seeking out information about other people's state of affairs, and searching and disclosing their secrets, has been strictly forbidden. (Hence, to eavesdrop upon somebody while hiding or pretending to sleep is like spying on others.) Spying, done with the intention of exposing the faults or unveiling the secrets of others, is a sin. It also leads to backbiting which is Haraam (illegal). Allah has closed every door that leads to the evil of backbiting and has made spying Haraam.

Abu Huraira (RA) narrated that the Prophet (S.A.W.S.) said: ***"Beware of suspicion, for suspicion is the worst of false tales; and do not look for the others' faults and do not spy, and do not be jealous of one another, and do not desert (cut your relations with) one another, and do not hate one another; and O Allah's worshipers! Be brothers (as Allah has ordered you!)***. (Hadith Saheeh Bukhari)

In our interactions with others, we should strive only for the positives. We should say what's good or refrain from saying anything. We should also have the moral sense and courage to stop others from backbiting, because, even if we don't contribute to it, we become guilty of the sin by being silent listeners and participants. The best means of avoiding it is by changing the topic or saying sensibly that we don't really know the whole truth of the matter so that we should not be unfair to anyone.

13.5 Resolving Differences with People

As long as we nurture any kind of enmity in our heart and prolong any conflict with a Muslim brother, we are giving evidence of the weakness of our faith. For faith in Allah is expressed through obedience to Allah. And Allah has said this in the verses of the Quran:

The believers are but a brotherhood. So make reconciliation between your brothers, and have Taqwa of Allah so that you may receive mercy. Quran (Surah Hujrat:10)

So have Taqwa of Allah and settle all matters of difference among you, and obey Allah and His Messenger, if you are believers. Quran (Surah Aanfal:1)

According to Abu Hurayrah (R.A.), the Messenger of Allah (S.A.W.S.) said:

"***The gates of Paradise are opened on Mondays and on Thursdays, and every servant [of Allah] who associates nothing with Allah will be forgiven, except for the man who has a grudge against his brother. [About them] it will be said: 'Delay these two until they are reconciled; delay these two until they are reconciled.***'" *[Muslim (also by Malik and Abu Dawud)]*

Whatever be our differences in opinions or feelings, we are expected to set them aside and maintain good relations with one another. Ego '*nafs*' is never to be allowed to supersede true faith. The whole purpose of our life is to prepare ourselves for the hereafter, and with this long-term goal in mind we have to overcome pettiness and trivialities. Our constant struggle is with two real enemies. One is Satan who keeps making the world and worldliness more and more alluring for us. The other is our own ego, which inflates our importance in our eyes beyond any sensible measure. It is these that cause conflicts and misunderstandings.

13.6 Controlling Your Hands And Tongue

How do we resolve differences that have unwittingly or even intentionally cropped up between us and others? The best way is to control our tongues and hands, which might be all too eager to express those feelings! Discretion in speech and actions is the hallmark of a sensible person. We need to consciously practice patience; we need to learn to talk to ourselves, to introspect, before we give freedom to our tongue and allow it to have its way. Particularly when it comes to speaking about others or voicing our opinion about them, we need to be extra careful that we don't mislead anyone. Speaking thoughtlessly, or on hearsay, amounts to slander, and we have been strictly warned against this. Allah Says:

"And those who abuse believing men and women, when they have not merited it, bear the weight of slander and clear wrongdoing." Quran (Surah Al-Ahzaab:58)

13.7 Attributing Positive Motives To Others' Actions

We could avoid slander if we could cultivate the habit of thinking well of others, so that even when we hear something negative about them, we don't just get carried away by it, but try to see the other side of the picture or story. Attributing positive motives to others' actions helps in understanding them better. Let us also remind ourselves whenever we attempt to judge others, that no one is perfect. We too have our own drawbacks which we wouldn't like being mentioned or discussed. Hence, fairness requires that we do unto others what we expect them to do to us. Moreover, we have been assured the protection and covering of our faults by Allah the Most Merciful on the Day of Judgment, if we are careful in covering the faults of a Muslim brother / sister here on earth.

13.8 Expressing Gratitude To Others

Expressing gratitude for favors done and help rendered is not only the basic requirement of social etiquette, but has other far reaching effects. It strengthens our relationship and adds warmth to it. On the other hand, taking others for granted, however close the relationship might be, causes disappointment and conveys the impression that we don't value people and that we just know how to use them. Gratitude and appreciation expressed sincerely with a smile emits a bright glow which is felt by the heart.

13.9 Smiling At Others Is Charity

Allah All Knowing considers smiling at others a charity. We know very well what a smile can convey – absence of ill feeling, acceptance, warmth, and the willingness to share our time or space. Let us not be miserly about brightening our face with a cheerful smile.

13.10 Visiting The Sick

Great merit has been attached to the act of visiting the sick. The Prophet (S.A.W.S.) showed concern for a (Jewish) woman who'd throw waste on him whenever he passed her house. The day she failed to throw it, he enquired about her and came to know that she was sick. He tended to her through her sickness and when she recovered she instantly accepted Islam.

13.11 Being Kind, Gentle, Caring And Concerned

The prophet (S.A.W.S.) has given us excellent examples of forgiveness, kindness and tenderness. An old woman - who intended to leave Makkah since she did not like the idea of a new religion being preached by a young man named "Muhammad" - didn't realize that he was the one helping her by carrying her belongings, and accompanying her till the outskirts of the city. Complaining all the way about a new faith being preached, which required giving up old customs and practices, she finally asked the Prophet his name just before parting. On coming to know that this was the man on whose account she was about to leave Makkah, she not only retraced her steps and changed her decision of leaving, but also accepted Islam, as a direct result of seeing its exemplary representative and a living ideal!

In conclusion, it is easy to see that bad habits picked up over the years in dealing with people can sometimes be difficult to let go of. Many times they may not even seem that bad, and this can lead to our overlooking them. However, we need to strive to change the undesirable aspects of our character and behavior, so that our families, friends, peers, and others can see the better part of us.

-- End

14. Using "Tawakkul" to Relieve our Anxieties and Worries

'Tawakkul' refers to putting your trust in Allah – to believe that He alone can ward off the harms of this world; provide you blessings and sustenance; and ease your challenges. Tawakkul is also about accepting the results that He decides, regardless of how they may turn out to be.

To understand the concept of Tawakkul, consider how tense and worried you get at times about the challenges of this worldly life. Whether you are worrying about losing your job or sustenance, or are upset over general life problems that you may come to face, Tawakkul is the belief and the attitude that you have about putting your trust in Allah to take care of all your affairs.

Allah (SWT), says:

"*...And whoever places his trust in Allah, Sufficient is He for him, for Allah will surely accomplish His Purpose: For verily, Allah has appointed for all things a due proportion." Quran (Surah At-Tala:3)*

The Quran makes it clear that Tawakkul is not an option but rather a requirement. Allah (may He be Exalted) says:

"*...and put your trust in Allah if you are believers indeed." Quran (Surah Al-Ma'idah:23)*

He also says in the Quran:

"....And in Allah let believers put their Trust." Quran (Surah Ibrahim:11)

Don't Give Up On Your Efforts

Tawakkul should not be mistaken for giving up your own efforts, and thinking that somehow your challenges will get resolved. Rather, striving and working with the attitude that Allah will take care of your affairs and will help you in getting through your trials, is part of you having the Tawakkul in Allah.

Some scholars have stated that *"Tawakkul in reality does not mean to actually stop working and striving for provision, for Allah Almighty has decreed that we should work and it is from His ways that He gives people when they strive. In fact, Allah Almighty ordered us to both depend upon Him and to work, to take the necessary steps needed to achieve our goals, and so the act of striving for our sustenance is an act of physical worship while trusting and depending upon Allah is faith in Him."* (Committee for Research and Verdicts – Fatawa Islamiyah, Vol. 7, Pages 172-174)

Allah says:

"...So seek provision from Allah and worship Him (alone)." Quran (Surah Al-Ankaboot:17)

Shaikh Saalih Al-Fawzaan stated about this verse, *"Look for sustenance and do not sit around in the masaajid (mosques) claiming that you are putting your trust in Allah. Do not sit in your homes and claim that your daily sustenance will come to you. This is wrong and a true believer doesn't say such things."* (Shaikh Saalih Al-Fawzaan Haqeeqat-ut-Tawakkul (pg. 15-25))

This is obviously applicable to other areas of our lives as well, just as long as we remember and believe that His will is a prerequisite for our matters to get resolved and, that we accept what He ultimately decrees.

The scholars have also stated that, *"other than our efforts that we put in, a Muslim should also combine Tawakkul with other means, whether they are acts of `Ibadah (worship) like Du'a (supplication), Salah (Prayer), Sadaqah (voluntary charity) or maintaining the ties of kinship, or other material means which Allah has predestined."* (Alifta.net: Fatwa no. 2798)

Allah (SWT), also says in the Quran:

[There were] those to whom people said: "The people are gathering against you, so fear them." But it only increased their faith; they said: "For us Allah is Sufficient and He is the best Disposer of affairs" Quran (Surah Aal-E-Imran:173)

Benefits of Tawakkul

One of the major benefits of Tawakkul is that it can relieve us of unnecessary anxiety, worry, and depression which can result from the challenges that we may be facing. By believing that all our affairs are in Allah's hands, and that we can do only that which is in our control, we leave the results to Allah and accept His decree whatever it may be. Ibn Rajab Al-Hanbali said, *"the fruit of Tawakkul is the acceptance of Allah's decree. Whoever leaves his affairs to Allah and then is accepting of what he is given has truly relied on Allah. (That's the reason that) Al-Hassan and others among the salaf defined Tawakkul as 'ridhaa' (acceptance)."* (Jami' Al-'Uloom wa Al-Hikam: A Commentary on 50 Major Hadith)

Let us therefore strive to understand and internalize the concept of Tawakkul and to make it part of our belief systems. In doing so, we will notice that things will not only get resolved easier with His help, but it will also relieve us from the day-to-day anxieties and worries of this life.

-- End

15. Balancing Between "Tawakkul" In Allah And Our Efforts

As Muslims, we are required to completely trust Allah (have Tawakkul) in all of our affairs. We also believe that Allah's will can supersede our plans. However, this does not mean that we should not plan and work in accordance with what Allah has blessed us with in knowledge, intelligence, and free will. Common sense, as well as Islamic teachings, tells us that we are to fully employ those God-granted faculties thanking Allah for what He has provided us with, without feeling proud and arrogant about those abilities. We see an example of this from the Quran, from which we learn that when Prophet Yaqub (A.S.) sent his sons to Egypt, he advised them, as a precautionary measure, to enter from different gates of the city lest they be mistaken as a clan or a group and thereby raise suspicions amongst the inhabitants of the city. So, we see that even as a prophet, Prophet Yaqub (A.S.) took all the precautionary measures that he could to prevent his sons from getting into any trouble. However, later we also learn from Surah Yousuf in the Quran that his precautionary measures were overtaken by the divine decree.

Sheikh Modudi in his tafsir (Qurani interpretation) describes the matter of balancing one's free will and judgment with Allah's trust as follows:

"Most people do not understand how Prophet Jacob (Yaqub) was able to hold the balance between "trust in Allah" and the adoption of precautionary measures. This was because Allah had favored him with

the real knowledge. That was why he took all those measures which were dictated by common sense, deep thinking and experience. He admonished his sons for their ill treatment of their brother (Prophet) Yousuf so that they should not dare repeat it in the case of Benjamin. He took a solemn pledge from them in the name of Allah that they would take good care of the safety of their step-brother. Then he advised them to be on their guard against the dangerous political situation and to enter the capital by different gates so as not to give cause for alarm and suspicion. In short, as far as it was humanly possible, he took all the precautionary measures to avoid every possible risk. On the other hand, he always kept this thing in view (and expressed it) that no human precautionary measure could avert the enforcement of Allah's will, and that the real protection was Allah's protection, and that one should rely not on the precautionary measures but on the favor of Allah. Obviously only that person who has the real knowledge can keep such a balance in his words and deeds, who knows what kind of efforts are demanded of his human faculties bestowed by Allah for the solution of worldly problems, and who also realizes that it is Allah alone who has the power to make them a success or a failure.

This is what most people do not understand. Some of them rely merely on their efforts and measures and discard trust in Allah, while there are others who rely merely on 'trust in Allah' and do not adopt any practical measures to solve their problems. Neither of these extremes is beneficial, rather, a combination of faith and effort is required." –
Tafheem-ul-Quran by Shiekh Modudi.

The lesson that we learn from the above is that we, as Muslims, should have complete faith that Allah will help us in our endeavors, because, without His will and help, no results can come to fruition. When we completely put our trust in Allah, believing that all success can come only when He intends it to be so, we can earn Allah's pleasure. Allah tells us in the Quran:

"...Certainly, Allah loves those who put their trust (in Him)" Quran (Surah Aal-e-Imran:159).

In parallel, we should also use all of our God-granted faculties in every endeavor that we choose to pursue. As we know from the popular hadith that **one day Prophet Muhammad (S.A.W.S.) noticed a Bedouin leaving his camel without tying it and he asked the Bedouin, "Why don't you tie down your camel?" The Bedouin answered, "I put my trust in Allah." The Prophet then said, "Tie your camel first, then put your trust in Allah"** (Hadith At-Tirmidhi).

Finally, does the above guarantee that we will get our intended result? As Muslims, we should believe that Allah, as the Lord of the worlds, has far more knowledge than His creation, and out of His wisdom He may decide to supersede all our plans for reasons that only He knows. We should remind ourselves that believing in **al-Qadr** (Allah's divine will and decree) is one of the pillars of Islamic faith.

Allah says in the Quran,

"No calamity befalls on the earth or in your selves but it is inscribed in the Book of Decrees (Al-Lawh Al-Mahfooz) before We

bring it into existence. Verily, that is easy for Allah." Quran (Surah Al-Hadeed:22)

So, before embarking on any effort, remind yourselves of the following:

- Put your trust in Allah
- Use your God-granted faculties to put in your best efforts
- When it comes to result, believe in the divine decree (Qada wal-Qadr)

-- End

16. The Urgency of Personal Change

We live in an era in which the world is mired in great challenges. It is no longer possible to ignore the turmoil that surrounds us, be it the instability in many countries or the problems associated with the millions who are struggling to make a living. Whatever be the reasons that led the world to this stage, it's clear that a change is essential in order to get out of this chaos.

Our personal lives are not immune from this turmoil. Throughout our lives, we constantly struggle to correct our life's course so that we could maximize our share of worldly and spiritual fulfillment. The process of a personal change can help us in capitalizing those opportunities by embarking on a journey of personal improvement. We can do so by inculcating better Islamic habits and others, which are related to other areas of our lives.

Bringing lasting personal change, however, isn't that easy. Many of us give up trying. But since change is essential to get us out of our current states, we simply can't afford to quit. So, the struggle must go on until we find a way to overcome the barriers to personal change.

We may wonder why we fail to change. For those of us who have attempted to change, but have seemingly failed, and have not much to show for this attempt, the process can be frustrating. Understanding the reasons that lead to this failure can help us overcome these obstacles. Let us review those below.

16.1 Desensitization to Time

Procrastination is known to be one of the biggest obstacles to change. Psychologists refer to procrastination as *"the act of replacing high-priority actions with tasks of low-priority, and thus putting off important tasks to a later time.[1]"* Whether one procrastinates in worldly or spiritual matters, it has its consequences. Procrastinators falsely assume that time will be available in the future, which may not, of course, be true. For example, we see that in the Quran Allah mentions numerous nations who were given time to heed to His message and change. The ones who didn't were suddenly taken by surprise at their appointed time. Allah says,

"So, when they forgot (the warning) with which they had been reminded, We opened for them the gates of every (pleasant) thing, until in the midst of their enjoyment in that which they were given, <u>all of a sudden</u>, We took them (in punishment), and lo! They were plunged into destruction with deep regrets and sorrows." while they will bear their burdens on their backs; and evil indeed are the burdens that they will bear! " Quran (Surah Al-Anaam:44)

The message above couldn't be clearer. Allah gives us the time to reform ourselves. When we postpone indefinitely, we should not be surprised if our conditions worsen. Allah says in the Quran, *"Verily, We sent (Messengers) to many nations before you (O Muhammad).*

---

[1] http://en.wikipedia.org/wiki/Procrastination

And We seized them with extreme poverty (or loss in wealth) and loss in health (with calamities) so that they might humble themselves (believe with humility)." Quran (Surah Al-Anaam:42)

We should, therefore, urgently start facing up to our spiritual and worldly imperfections which may be manifesting as sins. Accordingly, we need to make the connection between those imperfections and our undesirable conditions. Remember, the price of putting off change can come in the form of tough times and future regrets. Let us not procrastinate until tomorrow, because even if we had the extra time, tomorrow could bring additional challenges, and could thus increase the already large load of our burdens.

16.2 Desensitization to Falsehood and Imperfections

Making a change of any type first requires that we clearly identify and recognize the negative behavior, habit, thought, or belief which we want to alter. However, when one gets desensitized to such imperfections, the need for such a change is no longer felt. The "negatives" become part of our existence and we become complacent about them. For example, many amongst Muslims pray Fajar (early morning) prayers after the prescribed time (or miss it altogether) and no longer see it as a sin or feel the impulse to correct this type of behavior.

Today, we live in trying times, in which we are driven by worldly interests more than the ones based on divine teachings. Many a times, we come at the crossroads of the lawful (halaal) and the unlawful (haraam). When driven by worldly interests alone, some of us cross into what is unlawful. Such an attitude is slowly blurring the lines between falsehood and truth leading many to regard matters of falsehood as truth. This is similar to the boiling water and frog analogy, which states that if a frog is placed in boiling water, it will jump out. However, if it is placed in cold water that is slowly heated, it will fail to feel the change and thus will never jump out, dying as a result of this slow change.

This loss of our ability to distinguish between falsehood and truth makes the Satan (Shaytan) sneak into our lives, further hindering our efforts to improve ourselves. Allah says in the Quran, **"And whosoever turns away blindly from the remembrance of the Most Gracious (Alláh) (i.e., this Qurán and worship of Alláh), We appoint for him a Shaitán (Satan/devil) to be a Qarin (a companion) to him. And verily, they (Satans/devils) hinder them from the path (of Alláh), but they think that they are guided aright!"** Quran (Surah Az-Zukhruf:36, 37)

Islamic teachings thus warn us against getting into such traps, and instead instruct us to never lose sight of the distinction between right and wrong. Just because we choose to ignore, rather than to rectify the wrong to suit our situations, doesn't make wrong as right. By maintaining that distinction, however, we can still expect to rectify it someday.

16.3 Lack of Commitment

Commitment to change is essential for any major change of attitude to have lasting results. Research has proven that things such as "will power" can take us only so far and for so long. We need a more stable "inner resource" to sustain our change efforts for a significant period of time.

One way to ensure that you stay committed to any effort to change is to clearly define the outcome that you envision from that change. Envisioning the outcome of a change is quite different from simply having the desire to change. Although desires may provide the emotional fuel behind our change efforts, they don't manifest the underlying complexities to drive an actual change process. Outcomes from the intended change must therefore be envisioned clearly, e.g. the new person that you will become after you give up a certain negative behavior, to ensure continued commitment levels. This visualization provides us with a definite point of focus for our efforts.

Take the example of the prophet's commitment when he started propagating the Islamic message during the early days of Islam. When the prophet's uncle warned him of the risks of doing so, he clearly stated, *"O my uncle, by Allah, if they put the sun in my right hand and the moon in my left in return for my giving up this cause, I would not give it up until Allah makes Truth victorious, or I die in His service."* It was that kind of a commitment that kept him going for the rest of his life, and which enabled him to bring about the change that he did.

To motivate us to do good deeds and to put our temporary stay in this life in perspective, Allah and His prophet have very clearly defined the outcomes of our actions in this life and hereafter. The detailed account they have provided us, about both our stay in this world, and after we take the last breath, shows us a clear path from now until our final destination. For us to make any change therefore, we should commit ourselves and clearly envision the outcome that we expect from our change.

16.4 Lack of a Personal Change System

Islam constitutes a system of obligatory 'ibaadaat' such as prayers, fasting, etc. that help a Muslim adhere to a discipline of maintaining his or her relationship with Allah. No one would disagree that if such ibaadaat were optional, instead of being obligatory, most of us wouldn't be able to maintain our current levels of spirituality. So, just as methodical and disciplined systems help us perform effectively in both our spiritual and worldly matters, instituting a methodical "personal change system" is equally important to help us follow through on the changes that we want to make in our lives. Such a system will help us to make, track, and sustain changes throughout our lives.

Finally, let us remember that to seek a change in our conditions we must do things differently from the way that initially led to where we stand today. So, the road from misery to fulfillment, from good to great, and from Allah's displeasure to seeking His pleasure starts with you beginning the process of change. As Allah says in the Quran: ***"Verily, Allah will not change the condition of a people as long as they do not change their state themselves" Quran (Sura Ar-Raa'd:11).***

-- End

17. The Necessity of Ikhlas (Sincerity)

Ikhlas (sincerity) in our actions and statements is of utmost importance for the acceptance of our deeds. Al-Bukhari and Muslim narrated that 'Umar said, "I heard the Messenger of Allah (S.A.W.S.) say:

"Verily, the reward of deeds depends upon the Niyyah (intentions) and every person will get the reward according to what he has intended."

Therefore, every action that was not performed solely for Allah's sake, is annulled and fruitless in this life and the Hereafter.

According to the scholars, there are two implications for the word *Niyyah*. One of them pertains to distinguishing acts of worship from acts of habit. For instance, there is a difference between taking a bath to remove impurity (to be able to pray and engage in other acts of worship), and taking a bath to cool off. Also, there is a *different Niyyah* for *Zhur* prayer than *Asr* prayer, and for fasting during Ramadan, in contrast to fasting in other months.

The second meaning for *Niyyah* pertains to distinguishing between the intention behind the act – if it is directed to Allah Alone or to Allah and others. This meaning carries with it happiness or misery and reward or punishment. For example, two different persons might perform the same act, paying equal effort to it, but one of them earns a reward while the other earns no reward, or even punishment, because the intentions were different in each case.

Some scholars have suggested that this is why people vary in grades (in the sight of Allah); it is in accordance to the intentions behind their actions, not because of merely fasting and praying. Imam Ibn Rajab said:

Know that performing deeds for other than Allah is of different types. Sometimes, this action might be to show off in its entirety, and thus, one seeks to be seen by the creation for a worldly gain. For example, this is the state that the hypocrites pray in. Allah describes them as follows:

"...And when they stand up for As-Salat (the prayer), they stand with laziness and to be seen of men, and they do not remember Allah but little..." Quran (Surah An-Nisa:142)

Allah also described some as follows:

"...And be not like those who come out of their homes boastfully and to be seen of men..." Quran (Surah Al-Anfal:47)

Thus, let us remind ourselves that showing off can annul our acts of Ibaadah (worship) and may even lead us to earn Allah's anger and torment. Sometimes, the act might be for Allah but also be mixed with the desire to show off. In this case, there are authentic texts asserting that if the intention of showing off was present at the time one intended to perform a righteous act, the act itself will be annulled and fruitless. But when the act was started to gain Allah's reward alone, but changed later on to include an intention to partially show off, then it will not annul the act, provided one strives to repel such thoughts.

As Muslims, therefore, we should worship Allah in sincerity and stay away from *Riya* (see an earlier chapter on this topic) and evil intentions. We know from Quran and hadith that Allah does not look at one's shape and wealth, but rather at one's heart and actions.

Performing a righteous deed solely for Allah can help us towards achieving states of *Ikhlas* (sincerity). This way, the act can be easily steered away from Riya. The Prophet (S.A.W.S.) said in an authentic *Hadith,* that among the seven whom Allah shades under His Shade, on a day when there will be only His shade:

" ...A man who gives charitable gifts so secretly that his left hand does not know what his right hand has given (i.e., nobody knows how much he has given in charity)."

In addition, Allah said:

"If you disclose your Sadaqat (almsgiving), it is well: but if you conceal them and give them to the poor, that is better for you. (Allah) will expiate you some of your sins." Quran (Surah Al-Baqara:271)

Scholars recommend that when a believer gives away charity for a good cause, he should not let his name be announced to the public, such as in newspapers, unless the purpose is to encourage others to pay for this and other charitable causes. Again, we should constantly be conscious of the fact that Allah always knows the real intentions behind our actions.

To conclude, let us ensure that we strive to clean our hearts, intentions, and acts from all types of Riya and instead should direct our good acts for Allah alone. The real rewards and payback is only with Allah and that's all that we should strive for.

Allah says:

Say (O Muhammad (S.A.W.S.): "I am only a man like you. It has been revealed to me that your Ilah (God) is One Ilah (God – i.e. Allah). So whoever hopes for the Meeting with his Lord, let him work righteousness and associate none as a partner in the worship of his Lord." Quran (Surah Al-Kahf:110)

Note: This chapter has excerpts from the sermon of Shaikh Salih Al-Fozan (Saudi-Arabia), **Source:** Al-Khutabul-Minbariyyah, vol. 2, p. 273.

-- End

18. Tips for Your "Muslim Marriage"

Every marriage – no matter how stressful, boring, or happy it may be – can benefit from certain tips to give it a boost. This article reviews two pieces of advice that you can implement for a better married life. If you are not married, you still can benefit from the concepts as they are applicable across the board.

The first reminder has to do with becoming cognizant once again about our duties, rights, and responsibilities toward our spouses, as obligated on us by Allah and His prophet (S.A.W.S.) What married couples often forget is that a marriage too, just like the rest of one's life's aspects, is governed by the laws of Islam. These divine laws were communicated, commanded, and taught to us by the prophet (S.A.W.S.) through the Quran and the traditions of Hadith.

So, the first reminder is nothing more than becoming consciously aware that the moment you entered in the contract of your marriage, you became obligated to respect your spouse's rights as defined under the divine laws that underlie that contract. Claiming ignorance about those rights, or your lack of resolve in upholding them is not, therefore, a valid excuse to not adhere to them.

The problem in this regard is usually two fold. First, many couples simply are not even aware of or knowledgeable about the rights that both husbands and wives have toward each other. It's not uncommon for many to rush into marriages with all the fanfare, but neglecting to learn Islamic teachings regarding marriage and the rights that husbands and wives have over each other. It's only when they hit roadblocks in their marriages that they start seeking those answers. Problems surface because each spouse assumes certain rights over the other, and each spouse's personal interpretation of what's right or wrong complicates relationships even further.

The second problem is that while many of us may take the time to understand how their partner is not meeting their individual rights, they often neglect to learn their obligations toward the other spouse. Driven selfishly, each spouse gets preoccupied with how their partner isn't contributing to the relationship, rather than realizing how they themselves are negligent in fulfilling their own obligations.

In the daily routine of give and take therefore, if your relationship is hitting hurdles, both of you ought to invest the time and effort to learn about those rights and obligations that a marriage entails. Use this reminder to make a permanent mental note to help you become conscious of how knowingly or unknowingly you transgress and violate your spouse's rights. Remember, you will be questioned about them.

Allah says about our obligations in general:

"O you who believe! Fulfill (your) obligations" Quran (Surah al-Maa'idah:1)

"And fulfill (every) covenant. Verily, the covenant will be questioned about" Quran (Surah Al-Israa:34)

"And whoever transgresses the limits ordained by Allah, then such are the Zalimoon (wrong-doers, etc.)" Quran (Surah Al-Baqarah:229)

Now to the second reminder – Every relationship is bound to have disagreements, resulting from day-to-day challenges which naturally arise in a family life, or from your spouse just having a "bad day." These should not be mistaken for a bad relationship. Relationships do not go sour because of these very normal issues, but rather because of the ways that couples respond to such situations. When the response to such situations involves disrespect for the other individual, cracks start appearing in relationships. This "disrespect" includes, but isn't limited to, putting down the other individual, disregarding their opinions, raising one's voice disrespectfully, etc. This then leads to a communications breakdown where disagreements turn into full-fledged disputes. When this escalates, small mistakes by one are perceived as crimes by the other, and just an ordinary "bad" day turns worse by spouses ending up in major fights – sometimes climaxing to a point of no return.

We should recognize that Allah created us humans, and that He has codified dignity and respect into our very being. Therefore, when we trample over someone leaving them feeling disrespected, we are bound to invoke an equal or worse response from our spouses, as well as sowing in their hearts the seeds of animosity, hatred and mistrust. So, remember that of all the things at our disposal that we may use to relieve stress or resolve a situation, disrespecting the other should not be one of them.

Both Allah and the prophet (S.A.W.S.) emphasized the respect and honor that we are entitled to as Muslims and humans. Allah says in the Quran:

"And indeed We have honored the Children of Adam, and We have carried them on land and sea, and have provided them with At-Tayyibat (lawful good things), and have preferred them above many of those whom We have created with a marked preferment." Quran (Surah Al-Isra:70)

During his last sermon, the prophet (peace and blessings of Allah be upon him) said:

"…your blood, your wealth and your honor are sacred among you, as sacred as this day of yours in this month of yours in this land of yours. Let those who are present convey it to those who are absent; perhaps he will convey it to one who has more understanding than he does." (Agreed upon, from the hadeeth of Abu Bakrah).

Abdullah bin Umro reported that he saw the Prophet Muhammad (S.A.W.S.) going around the Kaabah in Tawaf saying (to the Kaabah):

"How pure are you and how pure is your fragrance. How great is your majesty and your sanctity. By the One in whose hand is the soul of Muhammad (S.A.W.S.), the sanctity of a believer in front of Allah is more than your sanctity – His possessions and his life and we always think good of him." (Reported by Hadith Ibn Majah)

So, remember that a happy marriage is one in which couples find ways to tackle and resolve challenges, without being disrespectful to each other. You can have your tough talks as long as you don't cross the line and begin disrespecting each other. Remember that Islam's teachings never sanctioned denigrating human dignity even in times of war. This being the case, how can we, when we are in the supposed bonds of love, step out of that realm?

To conclude, wives can strive to become what the prophet referred to in this hadith:

The Prophet (pbuh) said: "The entire world is full of resources, and among them the best resource is a righteous wife." (Reported by: Abdullah ibn Amr (r) Source: Saheeh Muslim, Vol. 2, #3465)

And for men, the prophet had this to say –

"The most complete believer is the best in character, and the best of you is the best to his womenfolk." (Tirmidhi #1162 and verified)

Let us learn our rights toward each other and let us not be disrespectful to the other even when we are in tough situations.

-- End

19. Reinforcing Traits of Personal Excellence

One observes that in carrying out of certain religious practices such as fasting in the month of Ramadan or performing Hajj (pilgrimage), Muslims demonstrate an unrelenting dedication, commitment, and sincerity. Driven by their spiritual beliefs, it is not uncommon to observe worshippers in the month of Ramadan, for example, to achieve more in reward by setting and keeping to a discipline, without fail, for the consecutive 30 days. For most, procrastination becomes a non-issue. Enduring physical strain through long prayers, hunger and thirst during the day, and little and interrupted sleep schedules throughout the day becomes the norm. All in all, people show no hesitation in stepping out of their comfort zones, and through a positive mental attitude, focus and self-motivation, such stresses don't seem to deter them from attaining their spiritual goals.

Believe it or not – the behaviors which most demonstrate for the full month of Ramadan are the very traits which are required to attain personal excellence. People have accomplished more, tackled and resolved the most difficult problems, and become effective leaders, by espousing these very traits of excellence. **Why then, one wonders, do a majority of Muslims fail to achieve the same levels of excellence in other areas of their lives? Why is the plight of Muslims today only mediocre at best? Why do so many Muslims sincere and passionate in their prayers, fasting and other rituals snap out of the spirit of Islam in other aspects of their lives?**

A chasm obviously exists between how we successfully step up to excel in our religious rituals, whilst, at the same time, we otherwise choose not to do so in other aspects of our lives. Because, if we habitually lived by the same traits of excellence which we demonstrate during some of these religious practices, we would excel more in our careers, in our learning and education, our dealings with people, would enjoy exemplary family lives, possess great health and healthy relationships, and dramatically improve all aspects of our lives. If each one of us did their part to drive toward excellence, the plight of Muslims the world over will be much better than what it is today.

The answer to this "disconnect" lies deep in our minds, and is mostly attributed to our beliefs. Our beliefs, whether spiritual or otherwise, which are ingrained in our psyche, provide us with feelings of certainty and drive us to take the right actions. So, while the strength of our <u>spiritual beliefs</u> drives us to take the right actions and consequently to excel on <u>spiritual fronts</u>, the lack of such strength in beliefs that are related to other areas of our lives keeps us from moving forward. Therefore, when we hold weak beliefs (or none at all) related to our desired actions, we only do the very minimal to get by – a far cry from what is needed to excel in those areas. As a result, we struggle in our relationships, have lower standards of education, pursue mediocre professional careers, struggle maintaining a healthy lifestyle, and so on.

Beliefs propel us to take action that we otherwise would struggle to take. For example, how many chain smokers do you know of who can quit smoking for hours during Ramadan, which they are otherwise not able to do? How many brides and grooms do you know of who were able to lose weight a few weeks before their wedding, even though they were otherwise unable to do earlier? How many cardiac patients do you know of who were able to alter their diet plans and to maintain healthy lifestyles permanently after they endured a serious heart attack? In all such cases, something changes in their minds that makes them take full-fledged action without fail. That is the power of beliefs. In changing behaviors, forcing oneself to act without belief works only for the short term. Can you recall how many times have you forced yourself to get into the habit of doing something, but have reverted to your old way of doing things? How many times have you forced your children to do something only to see no change in their behavior in the long run? Quran also teaches us that the act of praying, for example, does not mean much in itself, unless one is grounded in the right beliefs. Consider this verse in the Quran:

"Righteousness is not that you turn your faces towards the East or the West (in prayers), but righteousness is the one who believes in Allah, the Last Day, the Angels, the Book and the Prophets." Quran (Surah Al-Baqarah:177).

So, if you have failed to see certain results in any area of your life that is because you must address your underlying beliefs related to what you have been trying to change. Simply forcing yourself to act for the moment can get you only so far.

Your beliefs come together through a combination of your experiences, knowledge, and the process of thought and reflection. Such beliefs also strengthen (or weaken) through the interplay of the same three factors.

You can probably easily see how the interplay of these three factors have shaped your spiritual beliefs. The exact same applies to other areas of your life as well.

We know, for example, that some of the beliefs that you develop through your childhood experiences carry forward in your life. Research done over the years has conclusively proven that children who are physically and mentally abused, become desensitized to human feelings, and unless other factors intervene in that upbringing, many such children become criminals. The repetition and intensity of life's experiences thus plays a major role in building associations in the human mind, and in the formation of various types of beliefs.

To have the right beliefs, experience must be coupled with knowledge. A "superstition" is an example where certain experiences help in the formation of beliefs without the foundations of knowledge. People in various cultures wrongly associate certain actions (e.g. black cat crossing a path) with certain results (bringing misery). Acquiring knowledge can thus help us to dissolve those superstitious beliefs. The more we learn about a subject and the more we increase our knowledge, the stronger our beliefs get related to that area and the more it can influence us to take on the right agenda for excellence. For example, if you start to regularly read and learn about maintaining a healthy lifestyle, you will surely become more aware of healthy eating habits, thus dramatically influencing your physical well-being. However, it is also important to tap the right knowledge in firming up our beliefs. In his book, Al-Fawaid, Ibn Qayyim said that *any piece of knowledge that does not make faith (belief) stronger is abnormal.* Any other knowledge, therefore, that results in misaligned beliefs can hurt more than it can help.

The process of thought and reflection (thinking, pondering, and critical questioning) is the third factor that guides our beliefs, allowing them to get even more powerful. Investing some time to critically question ourselves, engaging in critical thinking, deep contemplation, examining the facts, putting together our knowledge and experiences, logical reasoning and other such behavior, can help us in uncovering more wisdom that can feed into the strengthening of our beliefs. The key again is to take the time to engage in such reflection and thought.

The Quran, includes numerous verses to guide people to use critical thinking and questioning to help firm up their spiritual beliefs. Surah Ar-Rahman, for example, is full of such questioning and critical reasoning verses after each of which Quran states: **"Then which of the Blessings of your Lord will you both (jinns and men) deny?"** Quran (Sura Ar-Rahman).

We, therefore, need to develop the right beliefs for the various dimensions of our lives. This also means that we break through any limiting beliefs that may be preventing us from achieving our true potential. Consider the example of a cricket. When a cricket is placed in a closed jar, the cricket jumps and hits his head against the lid. After repeated attempts, if the jar's lid is opened, the cricket jumps no higher than the jar lid because that's how his experiences have conditioned him. This can happen to us. Through our experiences, if we have been accustomed to do only so much for ourselves and for everyone around us, we may have developed self-limiting beliefs that keep us from achieving our true potential. Seeking more knowledge and reflecting on it can help reverse this and propel us on the avenues of excellence.

Roger Bannister, the person who first broke the record in the 1950s by running a distance of one mile in under 4-minutes, stated, *"Doctors and scientists said that breaking the four-minute mile was impossible, that one would die in the attempt…"*. Yet, he first believed he could break that record and then practiced until he actually broke that record. Once he broke that record, many more athletes broke the same 4-minute barrier within a few months proving that wrong beliefs held in one's mind can sometimes restrict our potential. As Edmund Hillary, the first person to reach the top of Mount Everest said, *"it is not the mountain we conquer but ourselves"*.

Therefore, each of us needs to brush up on our traits of personal excellence that may be hiding within our psyche, and to bring them into other areas of our lives by appropriately calibrating our beliefs. Because, as we Muslims play the game of life by the rules of Islam, we need to do it properly. We need to remind ourselves that Islam is a complete way of life and not limited to the few rituals of praying and fasting. Given the right set of beliefs, we can espouse those traits of excellence and use that potential in all areas of our lives.

-- End

20. Islamic Morals and Etiquettes

Although Islam provides the foundation for Muslims to live peaceful and civilized lives, many amongst Muslims don't live by those guidelines. In this day and age, unfortunately it is not uncommon to hear all types of tragic cases. We hear various cases where Muslims exhibit behavior unbecoming of a true Muslim. In extreme cases, these behaviors include but are not limited to domestic violence; spousal beatings; child abuse; elder abuse; a lack of respect for parents and elders; spousal lack of respect; intergenerational conflict; teenage pregnancies, and so on. These cases are heard throughout the Muslim world including the Muslim communities in the west.

These painful stories beg many questions – Where is the real Islam in these Muslim households allegedly perpetrating such acts and social evils? Does the Muslim upbringing today lack an adequate focus on Islamic mannerisms, morals, and etiquettes, and instead focus merely on spiritual and ritualistic aspects (praying, fasting, etc.)? What can be done to train families and individuals on Islamic etiquettes, morals, and mannerisms?

Based on a general observation of an increase in social evils within Muslim communities, it is safe to attribute the root cause to an underinvestment in inculcating adequate Islamic etiquettes and morals in our societies and communities. Education and knowledge in Muslim households, like others, instead focuses mostly on career building. This realm of education in today's Muslim mind can be observed in Tony Blair's (UK's ex-prime minister) statement, in which he said in an interview (reported in the Times Educational Supplement of July 5, 2002): *"Education is and remains the absolute number one priority for the country because without a quality education system and an educated workforce, we cannot succeed economically."*[2]

No one denies the need for education, which is required to advance oneself economically and also for the betterment of life in general. However, the knowledge and education which is required to instill moral values must not be ignored. The focus today may be more towards the building of human beings into entrepreneurs, doctors, engineers and so on, instead of making humans beings human. As a result, a number of us are succeeding economically but the question remains whether we are truly happy within our families, communities, and societies at large?

Within the context of Islamic education, the Muslim upbringing today may be solely focused on spiritual and ritualistic aspects (praying, fasting, etc.), while ignoring the morals and values that these rituals are meant to instill in the individual in the first place. We all know people who may pray five times a day and fast, yet who fail to epitomize good Islamic morals and etiquettes. On a smaller scale, most of us in one form or another may be guilty of maintaining double standards ourselves. We stand to pray in front of our Creator with humility yet fail to demonstrate humility to our families and other people. We may read the Quran but our character is not that of the Quran. We exercise patience and restraint in refraining from eating and drinking when

---

[2] http://en.mfethullahgulen.org/conference-papers/contributions-of-the-gulen-movement/2524-a-station-above-that-of-angels-the-vision-of-islamic-education-within-pluralistic-societies-in-the-thought-of-gulen-a-study-of-contrasts-between-turkey-and-the-uk.html

fasting, yet fail to show any patience or restraint when it comes to worldly matters.

This sad state of affairs calls for the urgent learning of Islamic manners, morals and etiquettes by Muslims of all ages. Besides building the spiritual core within the young Muslims, parents must also focus on instilling Islamic values that can help guide the new Muslim's life in these turbulent times. For those of us who didn't get the opportunity to teach or learn those Islamic manners, we can start by reflecting the Quran and Hadith, taking the teachings, and more importantly by starting to apply those to our lives. A book by Imam Bukhari (**Al Adab al Mufrad – Muslim Morals and Manners**) lists more than 600 Islamic manners and morals, and is an excellent source for learning Islamic morals and etiquettes.

Finally, let us review some of the Islamic mannerisms from the life of the prophet (S.A.W.S.) and sahaba. Abu Haamid al-Ghazaali in Ihya' 'Uloom al-Deen highlighted the prophet's qualities, some of which are stated as follows –

- *He was the most forbearing of people, the most courageous of people, the most just of people, the most chaste of people.*
- *He was the most modest of people and would not look anyone straight in the eye.*
- *He would respond to the invitations of slave and free alike, and accept a gift even if it was a cup of milk, and he would reward a person for it.*
- *He got angry for the sake of his Lord but he did not get angry for his own sake.*

- *He would adhere to the truth even if that resulted in harm for himself or his companions. He found one of the best of his companions slain in an area where Jews lived, but he did not treat them harshly or do more than that which is prescribed by sharee'ah.*
- *He would accept invitations to meals, visit the sick, and attend funerals.*
- *He was the most humble and quiet of people without being arrogant, the most eloquent without being long-winded, the most cheerful of countenance.*
- *He would sit with the poor and offer food to and eat with the needy, honoring the virtuous and softening the hearts of people of status by treating them kindly.*
- *He upheld ties of kinship without favoring his relatives over those who were better than them, and he did not treat anyone harshly.*
- *He accepted the excuses of those who apologized to him; he would joke but he only spoke the truth, and he would smile without laughing out loud.*
- *He did not waste time without striving for the sake of Allah or doing that which was essential to better himself. He did not look down on any poor person because of his poverty or chronic sickness, and he did not fear any king because of his power.*

To conclude, let us remind ourselves of what the mother of the believers Aa'ishah (may Allah be pleased with her) said when describing the Prophet (peace and blessings of Allah be upon him). It is mentioned in the lengthy story about Sa'd ibn Hishaam ibn 'Aamir, when he came to Madeenah and went to 'Aa'ishah and asked her about some matters. He said:

I said: O Mother of the believers, tell me about the character of the Messenger of Allah (S.A.W.S.). She said: Do you not read the Quran? I said: Of course. She said: The character of the Prophet of Allah (S.A.W.S.) was the Quran. I wanted to get up and not ask about anything else until I died... Narrated by Muslim (746).

-- End

21. Living Islam Within a Family (Home)

Strong family ties built on the teachings of Quran and Sunnah provide the necessary foundation for a happy and joyous household. In turn, this foundation contributes to the overall health of a society. On the other hand, members of troubled families struggle to maintain calm within themselves, and watch helplessly as day-to-day troubles tarnish and strain their relationships. As a result, they must grapple with the daily stress in their lives. In extreme cases, this might result in the corruption of the very foundations of societies at large. As family members, therefore, everyone has the obligation to take the necessary measures to strengthen these foundations.

Having a family is a blessing, and its members must work to make family life at home peaceful and joyful. Allah says (interpretation of the meaning):

"And Allah has made for you in your homes an abode ..." Quran (Surah An-Nahl:80)

A home is also a place of protection from the fitnah (corruption) of the outside world. The Prophet (S.A.W.S.) said: *"The safety of a man at times of fitnah is in his staying home."*

Islamic teachings based on the foundation of the Quran and the teachings of the Prophet (S.A.W.S.) provide us with those guidelines for living a harmonious family life. To benefit from those guidelines, we ought to "live" Islam within our families. We do not become Muslims simply by being born into a Muslim family. Rather, Islamic character is formed from a combination of parental efforts, personal struggle, prayers and supplications.

The necessity to bring Islam into our families is underscored by Allah telling us in the Quran to protect ourselves and our family members from the fire. He says in the Quran:

"O you who believe! Protect yourselves and your families against a Fire (Hell) whose fuel is men and stones, over which are (appointed) angels stern (and) severe, who disobey not the commands they receive from Allah, but do that which they are commanded." Quran (Surah Tahrim:6)

Protecting one's family from the fire refers to fostering a guiding and supporting environment for our families. The Prophet (S.A.W.S.), too, stressed that we all actively help lead our families in the right direction. He (S.A.W.S.) said as was narrated from Ibn 'Umar: *"Each of you is a shepherd and each of you is responsible for his flock. The ameer (ruler) who governs the people is a shepherd and is responsible for his flock. A man is the shepherd of the members of his household and is responsible for them. A woman is the shepherd of her husband's house and children and is responsible for them... Each of you is a shepherd and each of you is responsible for his flock."* (Narrated by al-Bukhari, 7138; Muslim, 1829)

"Allah will ask every shepherd (or responsible person) about his flock (those for whom he was responsible), whether he took care of it or neglected it, until He asks a man about his household."

In Saheeh al-Bukhaari (7151) and Saheeh Muslim (142), in Kitaab al-Imaarah, it is narrated that Mafil ibn Yasaar al-Muzni (may Allah be pleased with him) said, "I heard the Messenger of Allah (S.A.W.S.) say: *"There is no slave to whom Allah has entrusted the care of people, and he dies neglecting his flock, but Allah will forbid Paradise to him."*

We know that the walls of a home have little to do with the building of healthy dynamics between family members. That usually comes from living our lives according to the principles of Islam. So, how do we live Islam within our families and nurture a good home? This article reviews six principles that families can use to live Islam within their families. This in turn can help in building the foundations of a joyous family.

21.1 Make Home a Place for The Family to Worship Allah

Let us start with the basics. Allah clearly tells that He created us to worship Him. That involves following His commands in our daily lives as well as remembering Him through various Ibaadaat such as prayers, Quran recitation, and so on. Within a family, we need to ensure that we are following all that is needed to fulfill our minimum responsibilities of worshiping Him, alongside helping others to perform theirs. For example, **Aishah (may Allah be pleased with her) reported that the Messenger of Allah (S.A.W.S.) used to pray qiyaam at night, and at the time of witr he would wake her up to pray witr.** (Reported by Muslim, Sharh al-Nawawi, 6/23).

The importance of family members frequently engaging in Allah's worship at home is evident through other hadith as well as the Quran. Allah says in the Quran (interpretation of the meaning): **"And We inspired Moosa (Moses) and his brother (saying): 'Take dwellings for your people in Egypt, and make your dwellings as places for your worship, and perform al-salaah (prayers), and give glad tidings to the believers.'" Quran (Surah Yoonus:87).**

In a hadith, the Messenger of Allah (S.A.W.S.) said: **"Do not turn your houses into graves ..."** (Reported by Muslim, 1/539).

One of the signs of a home that is filled with Allah's remembrance is for it to become lively at Tahajjud, Fajar, and other prayers. This habit alone can bring tremendous peace to one's household. The importance of this habit is obvious from a hadith narrated by Abu Moosa al-Ash'ari who said that the Prophet (S.A.W.S.) said: **"The likeness of a house in which Allah is remembered and the house in which Allah is not remembered is that of the living and the dead, respectively."** (by Al-Bukhaari (6407))

With regard to men, the Prophet (S.A.W.S.) said: **"The best prayer is a man's prayer in his house – apart from the prescribed prayers (which should be in a masjid)."** (Reported by al-Bukhaari, *al-Fath*, no.

731). With regard to women, the Prophet (S.A.W.S.) said: **"The best prayer for women is [that offered] in the furthest (innermost) part of their houses."** (Reported by al-Tabaraani. *Saheeh al-Jaami'*, 3311).

A home filled with the remembrance of the Lord will no doubt find an aura of peace and tranquility in its midst, one which it may not otherwise find possible.

21.2 Keep Satan Out of Your House

Allah has told us in the Quran that Satan is our enemy and we should do everything to keep Satan out of our lives. Satan hurts us by misguiding us toward evil deeds, making the bad look acceptable, bringing misfortune into our lives and families, and so on. The more we succeed in keeping Satan's tactics and curses away from our lives and our homes, the fewer will be the fights, arguments, misunderstandings, etc., and the more will we enjoy Allah's peace and blessings.

Both Allah and the Prophet (S.A.W.S.) have told us how to ward off Satan's whispers and other evil tactics. For example, when entering a house, we should ensure that everyone welcomes the others at home by saying the Islamic greeting of "Assalamualaikum". Muslim reported in his Saheeh that the Messenger of Allah (S.A.W.S.) said: **"When any one of you enters his home and mentions the Name of Allah when he enters and when he eats, the Shaytaan says (about himself): 'You have no place to stay and nothing to eat here.' If he enters and does not mention the name of Allah when he enters, [the**

Shaytaan] says (to himself), 'You have a place to stay.' If he does not mention the name of Allah when he eats, [the Shaytaan says], 'You have a place to stay and something to eat.'"* (Reported by Imaam Ahmad, al-Musnad, 3/346; Muslim, 3/1599).

Abu Dawood reported in his Sunan that the Messenger of Allah (S.A.W.S.) said: *"If a man goes out of his house and says,* **'Bismillaah, tawakkaltu 'ala Allah, laa hawla wa laa quwwata illaa Billaah** *(In the name of Allah, I put my trust in Allah, there is no help and no strength except in Allah),' it will be said to him, 'This will take care of you, you are guided, you have what you need and you are protected.' The Shaytaan will stay away from him, and another shaytaan will say to him,* **'What can you do with a man who is guided, provided for and protected?'"** (Reported by Abu Dawood and al-Tirmidhi. Saheeh al-Jaami', no. 499)

Another tactic to keep Satan away from the house is for family members to recite Surah Al-Baqarah regularly. As this surah is long, family members can alternate in the recitation of the Surah. The Messenger of Allah (S.A.W.S.) said: **"Do not make your houses into graves. The Shaytaan flees from a house in which Surat al-Baqarah is recited."** (Reported by Muslim, 1/539). He (S.A.W.S.) also said: **"Allah wrote a document two thousand years before He created the heavens and the earth, which is kept near the Throne, and He revealed two aayaat of it with which He concluded Soorat al-Baqarah. If they are recited in a house for three consecutive nights, the Shaytaan will not approach it."** (Reported by Imaam Ahmad in *al-Musnad*, 4/274, and others. *Saheeh al-Jaami'*, 1799).

21.3 Let Respect, Kindness and Trust Rule the Affairs of the Family

Mother of the believers, Aa'ishah (may Allah be pleased with her) said: "The Messenger of Allah (S.A.W.S.) said: *'When Allah – may He be glorified – wills some good towards the people of a household, He introduces kindness among them.'*" (Reported by Imaam Ahmad in *al-Musnad*, 6/71; *Saheeh al-Jaami'*, 303).

Each individual has a unique identity and individuality that deserves to be respected. Giving time to listen to each other and helping solve problems in the light of Islam will make a household more conducive to productive problem solving. On the contrary, a home filled with frequent argumentation, disputes, and quarrels will foster only bad feelings, and this is something that stands counter to the teachings of the Quran and the Sunnah.

Let us remember that the Prophet (S.A.W.S.) associated an argumentative and disputing attitude with misguidance. He said, **"A nation never went astray after being guided except by means of disputation** (Tirmidhi #3253 and ibn Majah #48 on the authority of Abu Umamah)." In this context, we should also exercise the use of our tongues with great care. The Prophet (S.A.W.S.) said: **"Blessed is the one who controls his tongue..."**

Family members should also uphold each other's trust and ensure that family matters stay private, unless there is a specific need to share it with others. This especially pertains to spousal issues and matters. The Prophet (S.A.W.S.) said, *"One of the most evil of people in the sight of Allah on the Day of Resurrection will be a man who went in unto his wife and she went in unto him, then he (she) disclosed her (or his) secret."* (Reported by Muslim, 4/157). There are other ahadith that clearly and strictly warn the spouses (likening them to devils) when they let others in to their very private matters.

21.4 Foster a Culture of Islamic Learning and Knowledge

Fostering and nurturing a learning environment at home, one where family members share Islamic teachings regularly, can help all members to become more knowledgeable about Islam, improving one's life in turn. Let us remind ourselves that the Prophet (S.A.W.S.) used to teach his wives / family and even servants quite regularly. Al-Tabari (may Allah have mercy on him) said: *"We must teach our children and wives the religion and goodness, and whatever they need of good manners. If the Messenger of Allah (S.A.W.S.) used to urge the teaching of female servants / slaves, what do you think about your children and wives, who are free?"*

Discussing Islamic wisdom regularly can help us to stay informed and involved in ongoing self-assessment. Most of us are usually preoccupied with issues related to our daily responsibilities, work, relationships and disappointments in life. While discussing these matters with our family members, we can relate them to how the Prophet (S.A.W.S.) and his companions resolved such matters. We should find opportunities to discuss such issues when everyone comes together, as during meal times for instance.

Family members should also use the learning opportunities at home to learn and advise each other on matters of halal and haraam. This can help us ward off Satanic whispers which are related to making haraam appear as acceptable. Let us remind ourselves that once we cross those lines and start characterizing the bad as acceptable, Satan further raises those limits and does not stop until he completely pushes us into the darkness of evil and shirk (polytheism).

Another way to foster a learning environment at home is for each family to instill the love of Islamic literature and books. So, beyond keeping a Quran and a book on hadith, the family should look to maintain literature on Quran interpretation and books of renowned Islamic scholars that can help family members get a deeper insight into the wisdom of the Quran and the Sunnah.

21.5 Make Family Decisions Through Mutual Consultation

Involving the family in important matters before making a decision ensures closeness among the members. Allah says in the Quran,

"... and who (conduct) their affairs by mutual consultation..." Quran (Surah As-Shoora:38).

Mutual consultation allows for each member to have a sense of importance and responsibility in the family group. Besides, when trying to solve a problem, the more brains that are involved, the better the chances for a solution. Problems can be resolved with one-on-one conversations between parents and children, and other family members. Rather than venting frustrations and focusing on the problems, family members should find ways to engage in conversations where solutions are sought in an amicable manner. Venting frustrations, blaming each other, harsh tones, and demeaning each other not only does not solve problems but also sours relationships and closes all doors for future consultations and trust. Let us remember the hadith of the prophet where he compared harshness with good behavior. He (S.A.W.S.) said, *"Allah loves kindness and rewards it in such a way that He does not reward for harshness or for anything else."* (Reported by Muslim, Kitaab al-Birr wa'l-Sillah wa'l-Aadaab, no. 2592)."

21.6 Understand and Fulfill Responsibilities Toward Other Family Members

Living with other family members also necessitates that each of us learns the rights of others. As Muslims, we should know the rights of our parents, children, spouses, siblings, and others. For example, Allah provides us clear instructions about kindness to parents. He (Subhanahu wa Ta'ala) Has instructed us in the Quran:

- ***And your Lord has decreed that you worship none but Him. And that you be dutiful to your parents. If one of them or both of them attain old age in your life, say not to them a word of disrespect, nor reprimand them but address them in terms of honor.***
- ***And lower unto them the wing of submission and humility through mercy, and say: "My Lord! Bestow on them Your mercy as they did bring me up when I was young."***

Quran (Surah Al-'Isra':23,24)

As we can see, the Quran is clear with regard to our duties to our parents. By fulfilling our responsibilities towards them we can also serve as a good example to our children in the practice of patience and kindness. Similarly, we should learn our responsibilities in dealing with our children. When parents recognize the child as an individual, address him and include him / her in discussions on general topics, a proper rapport is formed and the child finds it easier to obey them. Reminders could be given and situations that parents themselves were in could be discussed to help each other get and stay on the track of Islam. When parents make the mistake of considering themselves perfect (and their imperfections are quite obvious!) they lose their own credibility and the respect of their children as well.

This also applies to other family members. Knowing the rights of other individuals within the family can help us fulfill our responsibilities as prescribed to us by Islam, and can help us live Islam within our families.

To conclude, suffice it to say that the Quran and Sunnah provide us ample guidelines on various aspects of living Islam within a family. One article is not enough, of course, to cover the above topics in any detail. Examples include verses of Surah Al Muminun (23: 1-11), Surah Luqmaan (31:13-19) and others. When the elders and responsible parties of a household highlight the importance to live Islam within a family, and practice these virtues and manners, this inspires the children to learn as well.

Finally, let us remind ourselves that simply becoming knowledgeable about these issues doesn't help unless we live by these practices. One of the Islamic scholars stated that if faith (eemaan) was simply knowing the facts in one's heart, then that is similar to Satan's situation because he was very knowledgeable about his Lord (rabb), yet his arrogance and pride led him to become argumentative and disobedient to Allah, and in the process became the worst of creatures.

– End

22. Other Books by IqraSense

Note: These books and others are available at HilalPlaza.com

1. The Power of Du'a (Prayers)
2. 100+ Du'a (Prayers) for Success and Happiness
3. Jesus – The prophet Who Didn't Die
4. Inspirations from the Quran - Selected DUAs, Verses, and Surahs from the Quran
5. Summarized Stories of the Qur'aan
6. Healing and Shifa from Quran and Sunnah: Spiritual Cures for Physical and Spiritual Conditions based on Islamic Guidelines
7. Jerusalem: A Religious History – The centuries old Christian, Islamic, and Jewish struggle for the "Holy Lands"

DUAs for Success (book) - 100+ Duas from Quran and Sunnah for success and happiness

- This book packs 100+ powerful DUAs that are effective for people in tough situations of life such as dealing with difficulties, financial issues, family, health issues, making tasks easy, success, and more.

- Includes AUTHENTIC DUAs from the Quran and Hadith (extracted from Saheeh Bukhari, Muslim, Abu Dawood, Tirmidhi, Ibn Maja,...)

- Transform the way you make your DUAs by instead making the same DUAs using the same words that were used by the Prophet (S.A.W.S.)

- These DUAs are also recited by the Imams in Haraam mosques in Makkah and Madinah during Taraweeh and Khatam Quran in Ramadan and other situations

- The book includes translation and transliteration of all the DUAs. Easy to memorize.

- The book provides potential uses for each DUA

- These DUAs provide us real solutions for when we need them the most

- The final chapter at the end includes the best of the best Duas as they are from the Quran with an explanation of when various prophets made those Duas to Allah.

DUAs in this book are suitable for asking Allah for:

- Relief from debts

- Increase in Rizq (provisions)

- Relief from anxiety and calmness in hearts
- Ease of difficulties
- Blessings for self and family
- Asking for righteous children
- Forgiveness of sins
- Staying firm in faith
- Asking for a sound character
- Asking for security for family
- High status in this life and the hereafter
- Refuge from calamities
- High status in Jannah
- Tawakkul (trust) in Allah
- Success in this life and the hereafter
- Health and wealth
- Asking for lawful provisions
- Protection from persecution
- Refuge from laziness and old age
- Relief from poverty

- Protection from Satan and other evils

- and 100+ more Duas

"The Power of Dua" - An Essential Guide to Increase the Effectiveness of Making Du'a to Allah

This bestselling Islamic book's goal is simply to provide information from Quran, Hadith, and Scholarly explanations / Quranic interpretations to increase the chances of Du'as getting accepted.

In this information packed publication, you will learn answers to these commonly asked questions:

- Why should we make Du'a when everything is already decreed?

- What can hold acceptance of Dua? (Important question)

- What can help make Duas accepted? (Important question)

- What should never be asked in a dua?

- A complete checklist that you can keep handy and work on as a reminder

- Can Du'a be made in prayers?

- What mistakes do people make after duas are answered?

- What are the effects of Dhikr on making Dua? (very important)
- What role does Quran play in the acceptance of your Dua?
- What are the stipulations for acceptance of dua?
- Why making Du'a to Allah is not an option, but a necessity.
- Understanding the life transformational powers of Dua
- How Du'a CAN change what is already decreed?
- The benefits of making dua
- Allah's sayings with regard to dua
- What mistakes people make that make Du'as "suspended" rather than accepted?
- What are the mistakes related to the topic of Du'a that makes Allah angry?
- What happens when a Du'a appears to be unanswered?
- What about the wait in getting Du'a accepted?
- What are the times when Du'a is accepted?
- Which people's Du'a are especially accepted?
- What if someone asks Allah something that is sinful?
- How to Invoke Allah in Dua?
- What is the best position for Making Dua?

- What is the best place for making Dua?

- Du'as that various Prophets made for various situations, and difficulties that they faced

- and more....

Jesus - The Prophet Who Didn't Die

This book's goal is simply to provide information from Quran, Hadith, and Scholarly explanations / Quranic interpretations about the story of Jesus and the counter arguments in the Quran about Jesus, and other Christianity fundamentals.

The book will take you back in time and narrate Islamic viewpoints on the day of the crucifixion, the story of disciples of Jesus, Mary, Jesus's disciples and more - all from an Islamic standpoint. You will come to know about the Quranic verses that are specifically addressed to Christians about some of the claims of Christianity, Jesus, and more.

In this information packed book, you will learn the following:

- The story of the birth of Maryam (Mary) to her parents Imran and Hannah

- Maryam's (Mary's) mother promise to God (Allah)

- What Allah said about Maryam about her birth

- The story of the Rabbis, and Zakkariyyah in Bait Al-Maqdis in Jerusalem

- The story of the Jewish Rabbis' lottery about them competing to adopt Maryam

- Maryam's ordeal during and before Jesus's (Eesa's) birth

- The Quranic story about Maryam and the Angel that spoke to Maryam

- The birth of Jesus (Eesa) in Bethlehem as mentioned in the Quran

- Jesus speaking from the cradle in defense of Maryam (Mary)

- Ibn Kathir's depiction on how certain Jewish priests hid the birth of Maryam (Mary)

- Jesus's (Eesa's) teachings and how they parallel in the Quran and the Bible (Injeel)

- Ibn Kathir's story on Jesus's visit to the Jewish temple the night prophets John (pbuh) and Zakariyah (pbuh) died

- The story of Jesus's disciples in the Quran

- Islamic view on how the story of disciples in Christianity contradicts Biblical teachings and Quranic teachings

- Miracles of Jesus (Eesa) as described by Allah

- The story how Jesus (Eesa) was asked to prove his miracles

- How Angel Gabriel (Jibreel) supported Jesus (Eesa) to do miracles that many mistook as Jesus (Eesa's) miracles

- How Allah explicitly mentions that Jesus (being a human being) was granted some powers (through the Angel and others)

- A presentation about the strong affirmation in Quran on how Jesus (Eesa) was not crucified

- The Islamic story about how Jesus (Eesa) was convicted of crimes by certain Jewish priests of the time

- The Islamic story about how Jesus (Eesa) spoke to five of his companions about the crucifixion

- How Christian scripture too supports that Jesus was not God

- Quran's explanation in Quran about the Christian claims of making Jesus (Eesa) as son of God

- How Allah questions Jesus about him being worshipped by people

- The story about Jesus's (Eesa's) second coming in Islam

- The hadith about Jesus breaking the cross in his second coming

- Explanation on New Testament's contradictions about Jesus's (Eesa's) life

- and much more.......

ABOUT THE AUTHOR

IqraSense.com is an Islamic blog covering religion topics on Islam and other religious topics. To discuss these topics in more detail, you are encouraged to join the discussion and provide your comments by visiting the blog.